Death Valley

PHOTOGRAPHER'S GUIDE

WHERE AND HOW
TO GET THE BEST SHOTS

DAN SUZIO

Nolina
PRESS

All photos by Dan Suzio.
To license photos or purchase prints, see **www.DanSuzio.com**
Production Manager: Susanna Tadlock
Book Design: George Mattingly Design **www.mattinglydesign.com**
Maps courtesy of the National Park Service

ISBN 978-0-9846415-0-5

Published by Nolina Press, P.O. Box 5803, Berkeley, CA 94705

PRINTED IN CHINA

Front cover: The author's shadow at sunrise on the salt flats near the north
end of West Side Road. DSLR, 10-24mm lens at 16mm, 1/60 sec, f20, ISO 200.

Back Cover • **Top left**: An original twenty-mule-team borax wagon at
Harmony Borax Works. DSLR, 10-24mm lens at 17mm, 1/200 sec, f13, ISO 200.
• **Middle left**: A desert iguana climbs the branches of a creosote bush. 35mm
Ektachrome Lumiere 100 film, 70-300mm lens, ISO 100, exposure data not
recorded. • **Bottom left**: Mojave aster in Wildrose Canyon. DSLR, 105mm
lens, 1/250 sec, f25, ISO 200. • **Right**: Photographers gather at Zabriskie Point
to shoot the first light of day on Manly Beacon and the surrounding badlands.
DSLR, 18-70mm lens at 25mm, 1/45 sec, f16, ISO 100.

Pauline Esteves quote on p. 29 is from *The Timbisha Shoshone Tribal
Homeland — A Draft Secretarial Report to Congress to Establish a Permanent
Tribal Land Base and Related Cooperative Activities,* U.S. Department of the
Interior, May 1999.

Caution: Like any wilderness area, Death Valley can be dangerous. Neither
the author nor the publisher will assume liability for any accidents, injuries,
or other losses resulting from the use of this book.

This book would not exist without the help of the photographers, writers, and others who gave so generously of their time and opinions.

For their professional expertise as well as friendship, I'm grateful to Tim Fleming, Dan Granett, Sandy Granett, Jan Hitchcock, Treve Johnson, Jain Lemos, Alan Magree, Jerry Monkman, Zoé Newman, Mark O'Shea, Fred Setterberg, Francesca Suzio, Susanna Tadlock, Ann van Steenberg, Jacqueline Volin, and Angel Wynn.

Each of you has contributed something important, and the book is better as a result.

Special thanks to John Binns, who first suggested the magazine article that eventually grew into a book, and to George Mattingly for making it look beautiful.

Above all, I'm thankful to my wife, Libby Granett, whose support and encouragement over the past 33 years has made it all possible.

Contents

A desert iguana climbs the branches of a creosote bush. 35mm Ektachrome
Lumiere 100 film, 70-300mm lens, ISO 100, exposure data not recorded.

Introduction

I'm crouched on a black rock outcrop at the edge of a steep gully, my eyes fixed on a big lizard about ten feet away. Its broad head and heavy body are dark gray, almost black, while its thick, rounded tail is nearly white. It's a chuckwalla, about 15 inches from head to tail—the largest lizard in Death Valley and the second largest in all the southwestern deserts.

The chuckwalla turns its side toward me, showing the full bulk of its body, and lifts itself higher on its muscular legs. It performs a half-dozen pushups, then quickly scurries toward me, bobs its head a couple more times, and runs back to its starting point. I respond in kind—a few quick bobs of my head, then I extend my body forward and back again. The lizard's eyes widen. It takes a tentative step toward me. I crouch lower and retreat a little. Emboldened by my fearful reaction, the lizard moves closer, and this time it doesn't retreat.

We repeat the dance, and eventually the chuckwalla is less than three feet from the front of my lens. After a few dozen exposures, I slink away backward and we're both winners—the lizard has proven himself the alpha male, and I've gotten some great shots. Only then do I look around and wonder if anyone has seen me making a complete fool of myself, doing a mating dance with a lizard.

Death Valley—it's a phrase that has become part of our popular culture, symbolizing desolation, loneliness, a frightening and inhospitable wilderness. But Death Valley is more than just a metaphor; it's a real place as well, one that can mean many different things to different people. To a geologist, Death Valley is where almost two billion years of the earth's history are laid bare, ready to be examined and understood. To a biologist, it's a wonderland of evolution, where plant and animal species have found ways not just to survive but to thrive in

Desert gold at the edge of the Ibex Dunes. 35mm Ektachrome 100VS film, 17-35mm lens, ISO 100, exposure data not recorded.

what appears to us a harsh and unforgiving environment. To a hiker, it's a place to enjoy wide-open spaces, challenging off-trail hikes, and spectacular views.

To a photographer, Death Valley can be all of these things and more. In this book, I will try to show you what it means to me, and at the same time give you some tips on getting some great photos. I've been photographing Death Valley for over 35 years, and every time I visit I discover something new.

What's in this book

In the first part of this book, I'll give you some advice on photographing the landscapes, animals, plants, and historic sites that make Death Valley what it is. I include tips on how to approach different types of subjects and what kind of equipment you might need.

The second part lists more than 60 specific locations in and around Death Valley, with suggestions about what to look for and when to expect the best light. I'll also tell you how to get there, what kind of vehicle you need, how far you have to walk, and other practical advice. Some locations will include tips on lighting and composition—although a lot of that will depend on your own creative vision. The locations are grouped into geographic sections.

At the end of the book is a combination index and quick-reference chart that summarizes each of the locations.

What's not in the book

Throughout the book, I make one assumption—that you already know how to use your camera and are familiar with the basic vocabulary of photographers. If you are new to photography, you will still benefit from this book, but you might occasionally need to consult your camera manual. While I avoid using too much technical jargon, I do refer to such photographic concepts as depth of field, proper exposure, shutter speeds, f-stops, and occasionally a few more advanced ideas. When a concept might not be familiar to everyone, I try to give a basic explanation.

My best advice for new photographers is simply to get out and shoot. Experiment with your camera's controls and find out for yourself what they do. You'll be amazed at how much you learn this way.

Chuckwallas are the largest lizards in Death Valley. They can sometimes be approached but will often retreat into a crevice, where they inflate their lungs to make it more difficult for predators to pull them out. As with other wildlife subjects, patience is the key to getting a good photo. DSLR, 105mm lens, 1/200 sec, f10, ISO 200.

Equipment choices

Everyone's needs are different when it comes to camera equipment, depending on what subjects you like to photograph, what you plan to do with the photos, and your budget. If your goal is simply to get vacation pictures and share them with your friends online, there are some surprisingly good and affordable point-and-shoot digital cameras that will meet all of your needs.

For the more serious photographer looking for a basic outfit to shoot landscapes, small wildlife, and close-ups, I'd recommend a digital SLR and three lenses—a medium-range telephoto zoom, a macro lens, and a wide-angle zoom. Add to that a sturdy tripod with a quick-release mount, a collapsible reflector, a pocket full of memory cards, and maybe a flash, and you should be able to handle whatever photo opportunities you find.

I've written this book from the perspective of someone using a digital SLR or a 35mm film camera because that's what most serious photographers use, and it's what I've used the most. (I've also photographed Death Valley with a 4x5 view camera and a 6x17 panoramic camera.) If you're using another type of camera you might choose to ignore some of the specific equipment recommendations, but the basic advice, such as how to light a shot or when to use a wide-angle or telephoto, will be the same. And the most important factor in any photograph is the photographer, not the camera.

When shopping for equipment, you might assume that higher-priced lenses

What's in my camera bag?

What I carry on any particular day can vary depending on how far I plan to hike, what I hope to find, and my mood. On a typical day in Death Valley, here's what I'm likely to have with me:

- [ ] **2 DSLR bodies**
- [ ] **2 extra camera batteries**
- [ ] **Several memory cards**
- [ ] **300mm f4 telephoto lens**
- [ ] **80-200mm f2.8 telephoto zoom lens**
- [ ] **105mm f2.8 macro lens**
- [ ] **10-24mm f3.5 wide-angle zoom lens**
- [ ] **Polarizing filters to fit each lens**
- [ ] **Flash with extra batteries**
- [ ] **Mini softbox**
- [ ] **12" collapsible reflector**
- [ ] **Monopod or tripod**
- [ ] **Squeeze-ball blower**
- [ ] **Lipstick-style retractable brush**
- [ ] **Lens cleaner, tissue, microfiber cloth**
- [ ] **Map**
- [ ] **Compass**
- [ ] **Headlamp**
- [ ] **Digital voice recorder**
- [ ] **Notebook & pencils**
- [ ] **Water**

Death Valley's summer temperatures can be life-threatening; you need to take these warnings seriously. DSLR, 10-24mm lens at 10mm, 1/200 sec, f7.1, ISO 200.

make better photos (when comparing lenses of the same focal length and maximum aperture), and most of the time you'd be right—but that's not always the case. Before buying any new equipment, read some reviews to find out what other photographers think of it and whether it seems right for your situation.

There are several "super-zoom" lenses available that go all the way from wide-angle to telephoto in one lens. It's tempting just to get one of these and use it for everything, but keep in mind they're generally not as sharp as prime lenses, or even as sharp as zooms with a smaller range. You'll have to consider the tradeoff between sharpness and convenience, which is not always an easy decision. I've missed many photos because my subject moved while I was changing lenses. I often

carry two cameras so I don't have to change lenses as often.

Protecting your gear

Changing lenses can have other risks as well. One morning as I was standing on a steep slope in Wildrose Canyon a sudden gust of wind knocked me off balance just as I had removed a lens from my camera. Reacting quickly to keep from falling, I watched in horror as the lens seemed to jump from my hand and make a slow-motion arc through the air, landing on a rock. (Where else could it land in Death Valley?) Since it was my most important lizard lens at the time, I had to make a detour to Las Vegas and look for a camera store. Fortunately I was able to find a lens that, while not ideal, did a fine job for the rest of the trip.

Rocks, of course, are just one of the hazards to your equipment. You need to be careful with your cameras and lenses anywhere, but the desert presents its own special problems. Wind and sand are the most obvious challenges. Fine sand can get inside your lenses and damage the focusing mechanism. Some zoom lenses can be especially susceptible—as the lens extends, it creates a vacuum that draws in air along with sand or dust. When you remove a lens, sand or dust can get inside the camera and appear as spots on your photos.

There are no secrets to avoiding sand; you just need to be vigilant. I use a UV filter on each lens to protect the glass. I always have a squeeze-ball blower and a lipstick-style brush handy and use them frequently. I also try to keep my hands clean so I don't transfer sand and dirt to the camera (not always easy, especially when hiking or scrambling over rocks). I usually carry my gear in a backpack, and I'm extremely careful about where I set it down. If I need to open the pack on the sand dunes, or in any other sandy or dusty location, I hang it on my tripod. If I'm not carrying a tripod that day, I'll find a way to hold the pack over one shoulder while reaching in with the opposite hand.

Extreme heat can damage some equipment, and the temperature in a closed car can be very high even on a relatively cool day in Death Valley. If you must leave equipment in your car, make sure it's well insulated. Cover it with a sleeping bag, or place your camera bag inside a large cooler. If you use film, you probably already know that excessive heat can change its colors. Carry only as much film as you might need for the day and keep the rest in a cooler—but make sure you keep it dry. I no longer use film, but when I did I always left it in the original plastic cans, packed those in ziplock bags (10 or 20 rolls per bag), and placed the bags in a waterproof plastic container inside a cooler full of ice. For sheet film, I would use ziplock bags inside of ziplock bags.

On any shooting trip, make sure you bring extra batteries. You don't want to run out of power before the shooting day ends. If you plan to camp, bring a power inverter that plugs in to your car's cigarette lighter so you can recharge your batteries while you drive from one location to the next. A solar charger is another alternative. A laptop or portable hard drive is always useful, especially on extended visits, for reviewing the day's shots as well as making backups.

Food, lodging, and other services

Several campgrounds are available in the park, at elevations ranging from below sea level to over 8,000 feet. In addition, backcountry camping is permitted along many of the park's four-wheel-drive roads. Make sure you check at the Visitor Center or online for current camping restrictions. Your choice of where to camp may depend on the time of year and your tolerance for extreme temperatures.

If you prefer indoor accommodations, you can find lodging in the park ranging from basic motel rooms at Panamint Springs and Stovepipe Wells Village to the midrange Furnace Creek Ranch and the more upscale Furnace Creek Inn. Stores, restaurants, and gas stations are located in the park at Panamint Springs, Stovepipe Wells Village, and Furnace Creek. Outside the park, a full range of services can be found at Baker, Shoshone, Beatty, and other towns.

Getting there and getting around

Death Valley is located on the border of California and Nevada, about 250 miles northeast of Los Angeles and 100 miles west of Las Vegas. California highway 190 crosses

There are hundreds of miles of unpaved roads in the park. Be sure to inquire about current conditions before driving off the pavement. DSLR, 18-70mm lens at 48mm, 1/80 sec, f10, ISO 200.

the park from east to west, and several roads connect the park to other main highways. From the Los Angeles area, most people drive to Death Valley via I-15, turning north at Baker, or US 395, turning east at Ridgecrest or Olancha. From Las Vegas, the most direct routes are Nevada highway 160 and US 95.

The maps and directions in this book are meant for general orientation only and should be used in conjunction with a detailed map of the park. If you plan to stay on the paved roads, the map you receive when you pay your entrance fee will have all the information you need. Before you head off on any unpaved roads, however, you'll need a more detailed map. You can find several choices at the Visitor Center or buy maps online before your trip. According to the National Park Service, you should not use your car's GPS to navigate in or around Death Valley — it's likely to include roads that are unpaved, impassable, or just plain nonexistent.

In fact, as GPS has become more widely used, there has been an increase in the number of people getting lost or stuck on backcountry roads, sometimes with disastrous results. Recent news stories have described a driver who followed her car's GPS directions down a closed dirt road and became stuck in deep sand for five days. She was found by a park ranger only after her six-year-old son had died of dehydration. In 1996, four German tourists in a rented van got lost in Butte Valley; their bodies weren't found until 2009. Park rangers have started calling the phenomenon "death by GPS."

Driving anywhere in Death Valley usually takes longer than you expect. The paved roads are narrow and often winding, with speed limits of 45 mph or less. On unpaved roads, the speed limits are largely self-enforcing: you can rarely exceed 30 mph and will often find yourself slowing to 5 or 10 mph. And besides, you're a photographer. You know you'll be making unplanned stops wherever you find good light, so you might as well build that extra time into your schedule.

My descriptions of road conditions are necessarily a little vague. I can tell you which roads are paved and which are not, and I can say whether an unpaved road is consistently rough or usually requires four-wheel drive, but some of the roads can change dramatically from year to year depending on recent rains, flash floods, and the Park Service budget. Before you travel on any unpaved road,

check at the Visitor Center or online for current conditions.

The Park Service, when reporting road conditions, tends to err on the side of caution. Many park visitors have little or no experience with driving on unpaved roads and may not understand the potential problems. The park rangers don't want to spend their ever more limited taxpayer-funded resources on rescuing people from their own lack of common sense. For that reason, most backcountry roads are closed in summer.

You need to take the Park Service recommendations seriously and understand that traveling on rough backcountry roads without the appropriate vehicle can be very risky. If you damage your steering, or have more flat tires than you have spares, or just get stuck in the sand, it could be days before someone finds you. And when you do get out, you could be facing an extremely expensive towing bill that your insurance is not likely to cover. Ultimately, your choice of vehicle will depend on your driving skills (which may not be as good as you think, if you haven't done much off-road driving), the condition of your car (also not as good as you think), and your tolerance for risk (inversely proportional to your age).

Use common sense as well when you stop your car. The most popular locations have turnouts or parking lots, and most of the paved roads have wide enough shoulders that you can pull over. But if there's no room to park safely and without blocking traffic, don't. Park somewhere else and walk back. On unpaved backcountry roads there won't

Average temperatures and precipitation at Furnace Creek

Temperature will be 3 to 5 degrees lower for each 1,000 feet of elevation

	Jan	Feb	Mar	Apr	May
High	65° F	72° F	80° F	90° F	99° F
	18° C	22° C	27° C	32° C	37° C
Low	39° F	46° F	53° F	62° F	71° F
	4° C	8° C	12° C	17° C	22° C
Precipitation	.27"	.35"	.25"	.12"	.08"
	.7 cm	.9 cm	.6 cm	.3 cm	.2 cm

Source: National Park Service

usually be any turnouts at all, so you just need to find a place where the road is wide enough for other cars to pass.

When you hike off trail it's a good idea to carry a compass, or, if you insist, a handheld GPS that can record your route and give you a return route back to your starting point. Don't rely on GPS exclusively, however—if the batteries die or it can't receive a signal, you'll be lost. Carry a map (and use it), and pay attention to where you're going and how you expect to get back.

While I do have a GPS, I generally use it only to record specific locations. For navigation I prefer the compass. A compass won't give you an explicit route, but with practice you can learn to use it effectively. It also has no batteries to wear out, it's lighter, and unless you step on it or happen to carry a

big magnet in your pocket it's not going to malfunction. Whichever you choose, it's not enough just to carry it—you have to know how to use it. Death Valley is not the place to take it out of the box for the first time.

Weather and climate

You probably know Death Valley is hot, but you might still be wondering what that means in terms of when you should visit. How hot are the summers? The numbers can be astounding. In 2001, the temperature reached 100° F or higher on 154 consecutive days. In the summer of 1996 there were 105 days over 110° F—and 40 days over 120° F. The record high, set in 1913, is 134° F. Yeah, it gets hot.

On the other hand, keep in mind that

Jun	Jul	Aug	Sep	Oct	Nov	Dec
109° F	115° F	113° F	106° F	92° F	76° F	65° F
43° C	46° C	45° C	41° C	33° C	24° C	18° C
80° F	88° F	85° F	75° F	62° F	48° F	39° F
27° C	31° C	29° C	24° C	17° C	9° C	4° C
.04"	.11"	.10"	.14"	.11"	.18"	.19"
.1 cm	.3 cm	.3 cm	.4 cm	.3 cm	.5 cm	.5 cm

these temperatures, and the averages in the chart above, were recorded at Furnace Creek, about 200 feet below sea level. In the surrounding mountains and canyons, the temperature will be three to five degrees lower for each 1,000 feet of elevation. So it's often possible to find a comfortable, or at least tolerable, location in the park even in summer.

Winter and early spring have the most comfortable weather, and that's when most people visit the park. The busiest times tend to be holiday weekends from November through February. Spring break also brings a flood of visitors, including field classes from many colleges, because it coincides with the flower season. During the summer months most Americans stay away, but the Europeans keep coming. I don't know if that's because it's the only time they have available for vacation, or because they want to experience the valley's infamous high temperatures. Whatever the reason, summer in Death Valley seems especially popular among Germans.

There's no real "rainy season" in Death Valley, and blue skies are common throughout the year. Even the winter months, on average, have very little precipitation. Averages can be misleading, however, because the total rainfall can vary so much from year to year. One big storm can bring a year's worth of rain in a single day. Two storms in the summer of 2004 dumped so much rain that the resulting flash floods buried 11 miles of park roads under tons of mud and rock. Fortunately, those events are rare.

Venomous snakes, such as this sidewinder, are often just out of sight under a rock or bush. Never put your hands or feet where you can't see them. To light this shot, I held a small reflector beside the camera and spot metered on the snake. DSLR, 105mm lens, 1/125 sec, f9, ISO 200.

Staying alive

For the unprepared, Death Valley can be a dangerous place. In addition to the high temperatures, the landscape includes cactus, loose rocks, steep cliffs, and abandoned mine shafts. And don't forget the venomous snakes, scorpions, various stinging and biting insects, and the occasional mountain lion. Seriously, you need to be careful. You should always have a first aid kit in your car—sooner or later you're going to need it.

If you've never been here before, it may be hard to grasp just how dry Death Valley is. Think about it this way: the (potential) evaporation rate at Furnace Creek is around 150 inches a year—while the average rainfall is

less than two inches. Dehydration can happen very quickly, especially when it's windy. A good rule of thumb is to bring a gallon of water for each day of your visit, or more if you're camping.

You should not try to hike here if you're not in good physical condition. Wear a hat, use sunscreen, and always carry extra water, even if you're only going for a short walk. I usually have one or two quart bottles with me, and up to four quarts for long hikes. You may be tempted to wear shorts and a tank top, but all that exposed skin can lead to dehydration, sunburn, and longer-term effects of too much sun. Lightweight long pants and a loose-fitting long-sleeved shirt will keep you more comfortable in the long run.

Wear sturdy hiking shoes, not sneakers or sandals, and pay careful attention to where you step. Avoid brushing against bushes or stepping close to large rocks that you can't see under. And always, always watch where you put your hands. Don't reach up onto rock ledges that you can't see, or you may disturb a basking rattlesnake. I've been handling snakes all my life, and I'm not embarrassed to say that when I look up and see a rattlesnake two feet in front of my face it always makes me jump—but I'd rather see it than feel it.

Before traveling on any unpaved road, fill your gas tank, check the air in your tires (including the spare), and ask at the ranger station about current conditions. It's always good to have extra water for the car—overheating is common in the spring, summer, and fall. You should also let someone know where you're going and when you expect to return. Cell phones don't generally have reception here.

Most of all, remember this: The roads and developed areas of Death Valley may be full of tourists and park rangers, but the wilderness begins where the pavement ends. You—not the National Park Service—are responsible for your own safety.

If I haven't been there, it's not in the book

I have personally visited and photographed every location in this book—some of them only once or twice, and others year after year for decades. The opinions are mine, and so are the mistakes. When you find those mistakes, please tell me about them! If you have any comments or experiences you'd like to share, or favorite locations you'd like to see in the next edition of this book, get in touch with me at www.DeathValleyPhotographers Guide.com.

Happy shooting!

Death Valley is a beautiful, awe-inspiring place, and you want to come home with photos to match. No matter what kind of camera you use, from the simplest point-and-shoot to the most expensive Nikon or Canon, the advice in this book can help you make the most of your visit.

Landscapes

A story in the travel section of the *New York Times* once referred to Death Valley as a "mono-chromatic wasteland"—a phrase that always makes me laugh, especially when I'm shooting at Zabriskie Point (p. 77), Mosaic Canyon (p. 62), Panamint Dunes (p. 107), or just about any other location in or around the park. The constantly changing colors, textures, shapes, and shadows make Death Valley a landscape photographer's paradise.

If you're visiting Death Valley for the first time, and you only have a day or two, there are three places you shouldn't miss: Badwater (p. 86), Zabriskie Point (p. 77), and the sand dunes at Mesquite Flat (p. 63). You'll see more people in those locations than anywhere else in the park (except maybe the shopping and dining areas at Furnace Creek Ranch), but go anyway. Stay in the park a little longer and you'll soon discover that Death Valley's sheer size and di-versity of landscapes and habitats can fill as many days as you have available.

Sand Dunes

Ask the average person to picture a desert, and chances are they'll think of sand dunes—not realizing that less than one percent of the land in Death Valley and the surrounding deserts is covered in sand. But sand dunes get more attention than the rest of the desert, probably because they offer so many photo opportunities.

Dune formation depends primarily on two factors: a source of sand—such as a dry lakebed or riverbed—and a wind pattern that causes the sand to accumulate. Sand dunes

The colorful badlands at Zabriskie Point are especially beautiful at sunrise. DSLR, 18-70mm lens at 31mm, 1/40 sec, f16, ISO 100.

Salt flats near West Side Road. Placing the sun in the frame, with the resulting lens flare, can convey a sense of heat. The bright sun will cause most cameras to underexpose the scene, so I set my camera's exposure compensation to +1, effectively telling the camera to overexpose by one f-stop. In this situation, it's a good idea to bracket your exposures, shooting three or more frames at different exposure settings. DSLR, 10-24mm lens at 13mm, 1/125 sec, f22, ISO 200.

appear to be in constant motion, but in reality they're not going anywhere. Dunes are often found near the base of a steep mountain range, where the wind moves in eddies that keep the sand in one place. The most easily accessible dunes in Death Valley are at Mesquite Flat (p. 63). Other dune systems in the park include Panamint (p. 107), Eureka (p. 54), and Ibex (p. 90).

Hiking on sand dunes is slow going, especially if you want to get to the highest point—and really, who doesn't? Hurrying will only lead to frustration, as the faster you try to walk the farther back you slide. Often the quickest way to reach your destination is by a circuitous route, avoiding the steeper slopes and following the gentle contours of the dunes.

To photograph sand dunes, you'll want to be there in the early morning or late afternoon, when the sun is low in the sky. In the morning you're more likely to find undisturbed tracks of nocturnal animals and less likely to see human footprints. As you approach, pay attention to the direction of the light and the shapes of the dunes, and start planning your photos in advance—especially if you don't want your own footprints in them. For the most dramatic compositions, position yourself so the light is coming from the side, rather than from behind you, to emphasize the length of the shadows and the texture of the sand. Notice how each dune is steeper on one side (opposite the wind), with a near-vertical crest where, in the right light, the strongest shadows will appear.

Time of day (and weather) can make all the difference in a landscape photo. Artist's Palette, photographed at 1 PM on a cloudy day, looks drab. The same scene at sunset on a clear day can be pretty special. Left: DSLR, 10-24mm lens at 16mm (cropped), 1/200 sec, f14, ISO 200. Below: DSLR, 18-70mm lens at 48mm, 1/160 sec, f9, ISO 100.

Don't limit yourself to shooting grand landscapes with your wide-angle lens—shoot those, of course, but remember also to experiment with close-ups and telephoto shots. There's plenty of detail in sand, and as you move in close you'll find patterns that you might not have noticed at first. When shooting sand dunes in morning or evening light, experiment with underexposing by about ⅓ to ½ of an f-stop to increase the color saturation. Digital photographers shooting in raw format can also make that adjustment, or fine-tune it, using Photoshop or other software. Small adjustments are best, or the colors will soon look unnatural.

Remember that wind is one of the essential factors in dune formation, so you'll need to protect your equipment from blowing sand. Use a UV filter over your lens, and keep the lens cap on whenever you're not shooting. (That's good advice anywhere in Death Valley, but especially important on the dunes.) You might also want to wrap a T-shirt or a plastic bag around your camera to keep sand off of it. There will always be more sand in the air as you move closer to the ground, so be extra careful when you crouch down for those low-angle shots. And be extremely cautious about changing lenses. Use your body to shelter the camera from the wind—or don't change lenses on the dunes at all. If it gets too windy, you'll need to postpone your dune photography until another day. A friend and I once spent half a day sitting in the car at Eureka Dunes in a howling wind, waiting for conditions that wouldn't destroy our cameras.

Panoramic views

For a view of Death Valley that seems to go on forever, head for Dante's View (p. 79), Telescope Peak (p. 103), or Aguereberry Point (p. 99). From there, you'll get a better understanding of how the valley was formed and how it has continued to evolve. It's easy to see that water has played a major role in creating Death Valley. The valley floor looks exactly like what it is: an enormous dry lakebed, with gleaming white salt deposits and traces of narrow, winding channels where water once flowed (and still does, in wet years). You can also see how the alluvial fans, those piles of rocky debris spilling out from the canyons on both sides of the valley, could, given enough time, eventually cover the valley floor. With an average of less than two inches of rainfall per year, you can only imagine how many rainstorms, and how many years, it's taken to create these gigantic alluvial fans.

Naturally, you'll want to use your widest lens for a view of the entire valley—and you'll probably find that you can't get all 140 miles of it in one shot. If you like working with Photoshop, you could try making a stitched panorama. Make your tripod as level as possible, and choose a lens that will cover the height of the scene without tilting up or down. It's best to have the camera in the vertical position, to minimize the effect of light falloff from the center to the edges of the frame. Then make a series of shots, panning from left to right, overlapping by about a third of the frame each time. Use a man-

Shooting with a telephoto lens, you'll usually need some support to steady the camera and increase the sharpness of your photos. If you don't have a tripod, look around for something to lean on. This photographer at Mesquite Flat found an interpretive sign that just happens to feature one of my photos of a sidewinder. DSLR, 80-200mm lens at 112 mm, 1/500 sec, f11, ISO 200.

ual exposure setting so the exposure doesn't change from one shot to the next. When you get home, you can combine them using the Photomerge command in Photoshop. This is a simplified explanation of the process; for detailed instructions see the links at www.DeathValleyPhotographersGuide.com. There are a few newer cameras that will do all of this for you.

While you're looking at the wide-angle view, also pay attention to the details that can be seen only from a high vantage point: the shapes and shadows of the alluvial fans and sand dunes; the winding traces of water (past or present) on the valley floor; the roads, buildings, and other signs of human habitation. Zoom in on those details for some interesting and unusual perspectives.

Natural Bridge, one of the few arches in the Death Valley area. Finding the proper exposure in a canyon can be challenging. Often one side of the canyon will be in bright sunlight while the other is in deep shadow. In this situation, many photographers like to shoot multiple exposures and combine them using HDR (high dynamic range) processing. For this shot, I used a single exposure and adjusted the bright and dark areas using the Recovery and Fill sliders in Adobe Camera Raw, a component of Photoshop. DSLR, 10-24mm lens at 11mm, 1/200 sec, f13, ISO 200.

Salt flats

Standing in a vast, flat plain of salt—such as you'll find at Badwater (p. 86) or along West Side Road (p. 94)—you can really get a sense of isolation as well as relentless sunshine. To capture that feeling in a photograph, you might want to break the rules a little. Strong backlighting, lens flare, and including the sun in the shot are examples of techniques that you might normally avoid but that, used carefully, can convey a sense of heat and isolation in a photo.

Like sand dunes, salt flats have a lot of small detail; you'll want to get down on your belly and shoot some close-ups. For an interesting perspective, make some wide-angle shots from

Above: Strong sidelighting at sunrise or sunset creates dramatic shadows on sand dunes. 35mm Ektachrome Lumiere 100 film, ISO 100, lens and exposure data not recorded.

Below: Titus Canyon Road winds through White Pass in this 180 degree panorama, made by combining 21 separate exposures in Photoshop. DSLR, 35-70mm lens at 35mm, 1/200 sec, f11, ISO 200.

ground level, with salt crystals in the foreground.

Finding the correct exposure on salt flats can be challenging. Just like when shooting on snow, using your camera's automatic exposure setting can sometimes result in underexposure, making the salt appear too dark. If your camera allows it, try overriding the automatic setting to *overexpose* by about a third of a stop. Don't overexpose too much or you'll lose the detail in the salt. If your camera's display features an exposure histogram and/or overexposure warnings, use them to make sure you're not going too far in your adjustment. The ability to see instantly the effect of changing a camera's exposure settings is one of the great advantages of digital photography. (I used to spend a lot of extra money on film because of the need to bracket exposures. Now I spend it on memory cards and software upgrades instead.)

Rock strata and eroded badlands

The colors of Death Valley are most prominently displayed in eroded badlands and exposed rock strata. Here you can see direct evidence, expressed in a rainbow of hues, of the minerals that have drawn generations of geologists and prospectors to the area.

Some of the most popular places to photograph Death Valley's geology are Zabriskie Point (p. 77), Artist's Drive (p. 85), and Golden Canyon (p. 82), but you can find beautiful and interesting geologic subjects throughout the park. My personal favorites include the Last Chance Range near the Eureka Dunes (p. 54), Titus Canyon Road (p. 67), and Striped Butte in Butte Valley (p. 93).

For the best color, shoot west-facing cliffs at sunset, and east-facing cliffs at sunrise. Everyone loves to watch a good sunrise or sunset, but you can always tell who the real photographers are—they're the ones facing the other direction, where the colors of the landscape come alive with the warm, glowing first or last light of the day.

Canyons

Death Valley's many canyons hold surprises and rewards for anyone willing to take the time to explore them. You might find a rare flower in bloom (Wildrose Canyon, p. 100), some long-abandoned mining equipment (Warm Spring Canyon, p. 93), or even an isolated population of frogs or toads (Hanaupah

Haze can be your friend. A windy day in Death Valley can stir up a lot of dust, resulting in hazy skies and boring photos. To take advantage of the haze, wait until sunset and use a telephoto lens to isolate part of the scene. These two photos were shot from the lower part of Wildrose Peak Trail, looking west over Wildrose Canyon. Above: 35mm Ektachrome 100VS film, 70-300mm lens at 300mm, ISO 100, exposure data not recorded. Left: DSLR, 35-70mm lens at 62mm, 1/200 sec, f13, ISO 200.

Canyon, p. 92, or Darwin Falls, p. 106). Those are just a few of my suggestions and discoveries; I hope you will explore and find your own.

Canyons can present you with lighting and exposure challenges. They're often in shade in the morning or evening, so you have the choice of shooting in harsh light or deep shadow. Or there might be bright sunlight on one side of the canyon and shadow on the other. It can be frustrating—or you can learn to use the contrasting dark and light areas to create an interesting composition. In some cases, you might want to make multiple shots at different exposures and blend them using HDR (high dynamic range) digital processing. Explaining HDR is beyond the scope of this book, but you can find plenty of information about it online. For some links to get you started, see the resources page at www.DeathValleyPhotographersGuide.com. If you're shooting film, or just prefer a more traditional approach, a graduated neutral density filter can darken the bright areas and make it easier to obtain the correct overall exposure.

Mix it up!

Before you walk away from any photo location, take a moment to look around and see if you've missed anything. You may have been concentrating on one detail, only to discover there's a better shot in the opposite direction. Or the light may have changed, and what looked uninteresting when you first arrived has become a dramatic landscape.

Dune formation requires wind, which can damage your camera equipment with blowing sand. 35mm Ektachrome 100VS film, ISO 100, lens and exposure data not recorded.

Whatever type of landscape you're shooting, you'll do well to use a variety of perspectives. Use a telephoto as well as a wide-angle lens (or use both extremes of your zoom lens); position the camera higher or lower to change the perspective; and shoot some vertical as well as horizontal compositions. Whatever you plan to do with your photos, whether you're shooting for National Geographic or just sharing with your friends online, they will be more interesting if you include some variety—not just the overall landscape, and not just the details, but how they all fit together to show the complete picture.

Wildflowers

Death Valley's wildflowers have a worldwide following. Every year dedicated flower fans start watching the weather as early as September, hoping for just the right winter rainfall pattern to produce a good spring bloom. Web sites try to predict the coming bloom and post updates from travelers. The park rangers and naturalists post a daily wildflower "hot sheet" during the spring months, highlighting what's blooming where. And once in a while the conditions are just right to produce a truly spectacular display, with hundreds of species in bloom, entire hillsides and canyons carpeted with every color imaginable, flowers bursting out in places you didn't think possible. Those blooms, such as we saw in 1978, 1998, and 2005, draw the attention of wildflower enthusiasts, botanists, and news media from around the world.

Unusually wet years get all the attention, but in fact you can find something blooming in Death Valley nearly every spring. With park elevations ranging from below sea level to over 11,000 feet, the bloom lasts longer than you might think, starting as early as February on the valley floor and lasting well into June on Telescope Peak. If you're looking for flowers, it's important to be flexible. Don't expect to find vast carpets of color every year, and be prepared to try several locations. In some ways a dry year is more interesting than a wet year. You might have to hunt for them, but finding a few flowers or a single bloom in an unexpected location can be especially rewarding — and can make an interesting photo as well.

Flowers don't need to be perfect to make a good photo. To add drama to these wilting Panamint daisies, I stayed low and silhouetted them against the sky. DSLR, 105mm lens, 1/250 sec, f11, ISO 200.

How small is this Bigelow Mimulus flower? One way to convey size in a photo is to add a familiar object. It may not be "natural" but it gets the point across. DSLR, 105mm lens, 1/200 sec, f11, ISO 100.

Shooting in harsh light

In other chapters I suggest shooting in the early morning and late afternoon for the best light, but wildflowers are a subject you can photograph all day long—as long as you know how to soften the light to avoid excessive contrast. Deep shadows and too-bright highlights can ruin a photo, turning a beautiful, delicate flower into an ugly, contrasty mess. I always carry one or two collapsible reflectors that I can use to reflect sunlight into the shadows. That's almost always enough for me, softening the shadows and, with a soft gold reflector, adding a lit-

tle warmth to the midday sunlight. If you want to soften the light even more, use a diffusion screen—white fabric that you place between the sun and your subject—or a light tent, which completely surrounds the subject and acts as both diffuser and reflector.

You've seen, and may have shot, hundreds of photos of pretty flowers, but how do you make one that really stands out from the crowd? Strong backlighting can add drama and interest to a flower photo, emphasizing the color of the petals, the texture of the stems, or other features. Use a reflector to fill in the shadows, and then experiment with underexposing between a third and a full stop from what your camera's meter says is correct. For the best results, set your camera to spot meter on the flower, rather than averaging the entire scene.

Selective focus is another technique that can give your photos a distinctive look: use a wider aperture (a lower f-stop number) to limit depth of field and focus on a small area of the flower. Limiting depth of field can also avoid distractions by keeping the background out of focus. By experimenting with these different techniques, you can discover which ones you like and develop your own photographic style.

Wind and camera movement

Shooting close-ups of wildflowers can be challenging, as even the slightest breeze or camera movement can throw your subject out of focus. To steady the camera, use a tripod that allows you to get close to the ground. If your tripod doesn't go low enough, you might want to buy a second, mini tripod—mine has a minimum height of about three inches. Steadying the flowers is harder than steadying the camera. Reflectors and light tents can reduce wind while softening the light at the same time. You can often position yourself to block the wind with your body, as long as you make sure you're not also blocking the light. Some flower photographers like to use a "plamp"—a flexible arm with a clamp at either end. You attach one end to your tripod and clamp the other to the stem of the flower, just outside the photo. Above all, be patient. Set up your shot and then wait for the right moment to click the shutter. And if it's too windy for a sharp picture, give in to Mother Nature and experiment with photographing the wind, or at least its effect on the flowers. Depending on how fast your flowers are moving, a shutter speed of between 1/30 second and one second should give you some good results.

Depth of field

A big challenge in close-up photography is depth of field—the closer you get, the less of your subject will be in sharp focus. As I mentioned above, you can use that as a creative tool for selective focus. But what about the times when you want the whole flower to be sharp? When I'm focusing on a flower, I try to pay attention to the edges as well as the center, so I can find the camera position

Stream orchid at Klare Spring, on Titus Canyon Road. Using only existing light, the background is too bright and the orchid is too dark. With a flash in a small softbox, the light is more balanced and the overall exposure and contrast are improved. Top: DSLR, 105mm lens, 1/100 sec, f8, ISO 100, existing light. Bottom: DSLR, 105mm lens, 1/100 sec, f16, ISO 100, flash in small softbox.

that will put most of the flower in focus. If you can't get enough depth of field using natural light, adding a flash can allow you to use a smaller aperture. When you use a flash, you will need to soften the light. I often use a small softbox that mounts directly on the flash. For maximum control, place a light tent over the flower and then use one or two flashes positioned inside or outside the tent—in other words, set up a mini photo studio out in the desert!

Whatever you do, be careful not to damage the plant. Harming any natural feature in a national park is not only against the law, it's unethical, and it could contradict the reason you became a nature photographer in the first place. If you need to move a small stem or blade of grass out of the way, gently wrap it around another part of the plant, lean a stick on it, or just hold it with one hand while you press the shutter with the other.

Lastly, remember to add some variety to your flower photos, including vertical and horizontal compositions, longer shots as well as close-ups. You'll be tempted to try for the perfect bloom in every shot, but looking at

Backlighting can highlight details and add drama to a photo. For best results, spot meter on a dark area of the main subject and underexpose by a half stop or more. To be safe, make several bracketed exposures. Using a reflector or fill-flash can help light the darkest areas and avoid excessive contrast. Top: Beavertail cactus. 35mm Ektachrome 100VS film, 105mm lens, ISO 100, exposure data not recorded. Middle: Panamint daisy. DSLR, 35-70mm lens at 40mm, 1/125 sec, f14, ISO 200. Bottom: Creosote bush seeds. DSLR, 105mm lens, 1/40 sec, f22, ISO 100.

photo after photo of perfect flowers can get boring. Pay attention to the less than perfect flowers—wilted flowers on drooping stems, dried out skeletons of annuals, flowers that have been partially eaten by insects or lizards—and other stages of the plant's life cycle, such as buds and seeds. Look for unexpected flower-related subjects, such as when the fallen petals of creosote flowers accumulate in the ripples on sand dunes.

Wildflower locations

It's hard to recommend specific locations for Death Valley wildflowers, because conditions can change so much from one year to the next. A spot that seems perfect this year might have nothing in bloom next year. However, there are a few areas that stand out, at least in my experience.

Wildrose Canyon (p. 100) has always been one of my favorite locations for spring wildflowers, with more variety than I've seen in most other places in the park. Common flowers here include mariposa lilies, Mojave aster, chia, and prince's plume. I've often spent a full day between Wildrose Campground and the Charcoal Kilns, driving slowly and stopping for an hour or two whenever I see an area to shoot.

Greenwater Valley (p. 81) is another great place to spend a leisurely morning or afternoon photographing wildflowers. Make sure you inquire about the conditions before setting off on this unpaved road. In a good year, some of the flower species you might find include larkspur, phacelia, des-

Nevada goldeneye in Butte Valley. If it's too windy for a sharp photo, try photographing the wind. Experiment with shutter speeds between 1/30 and 1 second or slower. 35mm Ektachrome 100VS film, ISO 100, lens and exposure data not recorded.

ert gold, chia, evening primrose, tackstem, gravel ghost, Mojave aster, beavertail cactus, and, of course, the ubiquitous creosote bush.

Other wildflower locations that I like are Butte Valley (p. 93) and Aguereberry Point (p. 99). At the Eureka Dunes (p. 54) you'll find the endangered Eureka Dunes evening primrose, a large white flower that grows nowhere else in the world.

The location descriptions beginning on p. 51 include elevations and estimated blooming seasons—but remember, the conditions can change from year to year. The resources section at www.DeathValleyPhotographersGuide.com has links to wildflower reports that can help you find what's in bloom.

Ghost towns and historic sites

If you like Wild West history and colorful characters, Death Valley is the place to be. Ever since 1849, when a lost party of fortune-seekers stumbled into the valley on their way to the gold fields of California, people have tried, some with more success than others, to make a new life in this area.

Native people

Of course, the 49ers were not the first people to live here. Death Valley has been occupied since the end of the last Ice Age. The Timbisha Shoshone, named for the orange-colored clay they used as a ceremonial face paint, lived in small villages throughout what is now the park. They hunted bighorn sheep, rabbits, and chuckwallas, and harvested many kinds of plants. Piñon pine nuts and mesquite beans were an important part of their diet. They worked hard, and the land provided everything they needed.

Pauline Esteves, former Timbisha Shoshone Tribal Chairperson, describes what happened when outsiders began to move in. "Then others came and occupied our land. They took away many of our most important places … the places we used for food. The places we used for our spiritual practices. They didn't want us to carry on our religion or our ceremonies or our songs or our language. The names of our places became unknown to some of our people."

To survive, the Timbisha had to adapt to new rules and a new economic system. After centuries of living off the abundance of the land, many of them had to go to work at

Remains of the Cook Bank building in Rhyolite, lit by a full moon.
DSLR, 10-24mm lens at 10mm, 30 sec, f4, ISO 800.

Abandoned mineshafts are extremely dangerous—shoot from the entrance, but don't go in. You never know when one will collapse. 35mm Ektachrome 64X film, 35mm lens, 1/60 sec, f5.6, ISO 64, with flash set to underexpose by 1/2 to 1 stop.

The National Park Service now works in partnership with the tribe to ensure the continued protection of the park's natural and cultural resources. The new Visitor Center at Furnace Creek, scheduled to open in 2012, will emphasize the Timbisha's role in the valley, past, present, and future. And a number of economic development projects, inside and outside the park, are being considered.

Very few Native sites are available for photography, and many Timbisha would prefer that their most sacred or traditional places not be publicized. One site that is already well known and accessible is at Klare Spring in Titus Canyon (p. 71), where ancient petroglyphs can be found.

whatever jobs they could find. The new immigrants hired Timbisha men as guides, miners, messengers, and construction workers, while the women often did laundry and other domestic chores in the new boomtowns. In the 1930s, when Death Valley National Monument was established, the National Park Service set aside 40 acres near Furnace Creek as a residential area for the remaining Timbisha.

Many people are surprised to learn that the Timbisha Shoshone are still here. In 2000 the Timbisha Shoshone Homeland Act established a permanent homeland for the tribe, expanding and improving the tribal village at Furnace Creek. The village is not open to the public, and the tribe has generally kept a low profile—although that may be changing.

Ghost towns

Death Valley's more recent historic sites offer a wealth of photographic possibilities. Close-ups of weathered wood and iron, rusted mining and milling equipment, ruins of wooden or concrete buildings, abandoned mineshafts, old trucks, and ore cars are just some of the photo subjects you'll find.

The largest ghost town, and in its day the largest city, in the Death Valley area is outside the park, just west of Beatty, Nevada. Between about 1905 and 1912, when Las Vegas was nothing more than a railroad stop and a handful of tents, Rhyolite (p. 65) was a rowdy boomtown served by four stagecoaches per day. This modern city of 5,000 to 10,000 (no one is exactly sure) had concrete sidewalks, electric lights, and telephone service; dozens of saloons, gambling halls, and brothels; an assortment of restaurants, hotels, and stores; several doctors and dentists; two banks, two churches, two undertakers, a stock exchange, a school, a jail, daily and weekly newspapers, and even a monthly magazine. At the Miners Union Hospital, union members could receive complete health care for a dollar a month, while nonmembers paid two dollars.

Today, you can wander freely among the ruins (two buildings are fenced off, but the rest are accessible), photographing the remnants of a past life. It's a much quieter place now. Rhyolite is one of the most photographed ghost towns in the country, but on many visits I've been able to spend several hours shooting here without seeing even one other person.

In a remote area of Titus Canyon is the ghost town of Leadfield (p. 70). Unlike Rhyolite, this boomtown went bust almost immediately. Built on hype and exaggeration, the original plan for the town called for 1,749 home sites. That plan made a lot of money for its unscrupulous promoters, but the prospectors, merchants, and investors weren't so fortunate. A post office was established here in August 1926 to serve the new town's 300 residents—and closed a little over six months later, when nearly everyone had given up and moved on to look for better opportunities. What remains are mostly corrugated metal shacks, in sharp contrast to Rhyolite's multistory concrete buildings.

Mines and mills

At the upper end of Wildrose Canyon you'll find a row of enormous stone kilns (p. 101) that were once used to make charcoal for a silver smelting operation in the Argus Range, west of Panamint Valley. Plan on spending some time at the kilns; their shapes and shadows can be used for dramatic compositions.

Most other historic sites in the park are not so extensive, consisting mainly of mine or mill sites. One of my favorites is in Warm Spring Canyon (p. 93), where you'll find an old mining camp and some abandoned equipment that was once used to process ore. In spring, the contrast between the stark, rusty metal and delicate, colorful flowers can make some interesting photos. Warm Spring Canyon leads to Butte Valley (p. 93), where at least three historic cabins are tucked away in the wilderness. Getting to Butte Valley requires a high-clearance four-wheel-drive vehicle.

A petroglyph near Klare Spring on Titus Canyon Road. Photographing petroglyphs can be difficult, because they blend with the rocks and are often hard to "read" in a photo. Increasing the contrast when you process the image can help. DSLR, 18-70mm lens at 70mm, 1/200 sec, f9, ISO 100.

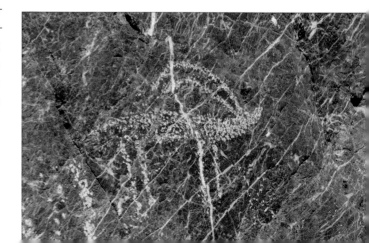

Using a wide-angle lens for this corrugated tin building in Leadfield, on Titus Canyon Road, conveys the sense of isolation that the residents must have felt. DSLR, 18-70mm lens at 18mm, 1/200 sec, f10, ISO 100.

Prospectors and con men

When I photograph Death Valley's historic sites, I always think about the people who lived and worked here, and how hard it must have been to leave their old lives be- hind and make a new home in this harsh, unforgiving desert. For most of these communities, water was a scarce resource, often piped in from miles away, and any wood needed for construction had to be brought by train or wagon. In fact, nearly everything they needed had to come from somewhere else, including most of their food. It's no surprise that the conditions here produced some memorable and colorful characters.

The Ashford brothers—Harold, Henry, and Louis—for example, dreamed of untold wealth from their optimistically named Golden Treasure mine. While they did find some gold, they spent most of the next two decades in court, suing and being sued by various investors in their operation. The remains of their mill (p. 88) can be seen at the southern end of the valley.

Frank "Shorty" Harris seems to have been involved in every major gold strike in the Death Valley area, but he never quite found the riches he was searching for. In 1905, Shorty Harris and Pete Aguereberry, a young Basque immigrant, found gold at the Eureka Mine (p. 97), attracting other hopeful prospectors. As Shorty repeated the story of their discovery, he seemed to forget about Pete, and the resulting boomtown became known as Harrisburg. After the boomtown went bust, Pete Aguereberry stayed on and worked the claim by himself. He must have loved the solitude and the work, because the mine never really paid off. In addition to mining, he worked various odd jobs to support himself. Pete worked his mine for forty years, until his death in 1945.

Walter Scott, better known as Death Valley Scotty, stands out as an eccentric even by Death Valley standards. A con man without equal, he had worked for Buffalo Bill Cody's Wild West Show before coming to Death Valley. Scotty claimed to have a secret gold mine in the Grapevine Mountains that produced unusually high-grade ore. His promotional skills and flamboyant, free-spending lifestyle attracted newspaper reporters as well as a series of investors, none of whom was ever allowed to visit the mine. The mine, of course, never existed. Scotty simply spent his investors' money on attracting new investors.

Even after he was revealed as a fraud, Scotty found a way to continue the charade. Chicago millionaires Albert and Bessie Johnson enjoyed Scotty's stories and continued to fund him long after realizing they'd been swindled. When asked why, Albert Johnson once replied, "I gave him the money because I got a kick out of watching him spend it. Scotty paid me back in laughs…" The Johnsons built a lavish vacation home in Grapevine Canyon that they called Death Valley Ranch, but it soon became known as Scotty's Castle (p. 57). While the home was built entirely with the Johnsons' money, Scotty boasted that his gold mine had paid for it.

To tell the story of these characters and the lives they led, I look for perspectives that humanize the ruins. Sometimes I'll stand inside a building (if it looks safe enough) and frame the surrounding desert in a broken window, for a sense of what the residents might have experienced. Or I'll focus on the details, such as the rusted cans and broken pottery that are scattered around many historic buildings. There are often interesting contrasts, such as a bright yellow flower blooming among the rusted ruins of an old mill. If you use your own creative instincts to find the photos that speak to you personally, you'll be able to make something original.

Wildlife

In spite of its name, Death Valley is teeming with life. If it doesn't look that way to you at first, that's probably because you're not accustomed to the type of wildlife to be found here. The most visible vertebrates, by far, are the reptiles, with 35 species of lizards and snakes represented. The park is also home to a variety of mammals, from the smallest mice and kangaroo rats to predators such as coyotes, bobcats, and mountain lions. And over 300 species of birds have been recorded in the park. Rather than try to list every species, I will describe some of the more common animals and how I approach them for photography. The resources section of this book suggests some excellent field guides, and in addition you can find species checklists online at www.DeathValleyPhotographersGuide.com.

As a wildlife photographer with a particular interest in herpetology, I've been in love with Death Valley since my first visit in 1974. To me, there are few things in life that can compare to spending a day out in the open desert, getting close to the lizards and snakes I find there.

It's all in the eyes

When I photograph wildlife, my goal is more than just documenting an animal's identity or behavior. I want to make a portrait, much as a studio photographer would, using the same creative techniques of lighting, composition, and color to capture the spirit of the individual as well as the species or location. In other words, I want people who view my photos to feel they're getting a glimpse of the animal's "personality."

This bobcat in Wildrose Canyon was unusually cooperative, but only for a few minutes. Then it disappeared into a stand of mesquite and I never saw it again. DSLR, 80-400mm lens at 400mm, 1/400 sec, f5.6, ISO 100.

A zebra-tailed lizard near Darwin Falls illustrates the importance of shooting from your subject's eye level. For the first photo, I shot from a standing position, looking down at the lizard while supporting the camera on a monopod. For the second shot, I sat down and held the camera on my knee. For the third, I was lying flat on my belly, resting the camera on the ground. DSLR, 300mm lens, 1/1000 sec, f7.1, ISO 200.

When I move in for a close-up, I pay careful attention to my subject's eyes. The eyes are key to a successful portrait, whether human or animal. When people look at a photo, they're naturally drawn to the eyes. The closer you are to your subject, the less depth of field you'll have, which means that parts of the photo will be in sharp focus while other parts will not be. Make sure the point of sharpest focus is at the eye.

Eye contact is also important—a photo will be more engaging if the subject seems to be looking back at the viewer—but you don't want to overdo it. The animal should look natural, like it just happened to look at the camera, not like it's reacting to the photographer's presence. In most cases the animal should be facing toward the sun (or other light source), so its face is well lit and any shadows fall toward its tail.

A little reflection in the eye, whether from the sun or a fill-flash, can be the difference between a tired-looking animal and one that appears alert and full of life. And finally, whenever possible, shoot from your subject's eye level or close to it. Avoid shots where you're looking up or down at a steep angle. Instead, either get down on your belly or start climbing—whatever it takes to meet the animal at its own level, in its own world.

Equipment for wildlife photography

When shooting wildlife, you often need to react quickly while at the same time taking

Many lizards, such as this side-blotched lizard near Saratoga Spring, are active during the harsh light of midday, which can add excessive contrast to a photo. To soften the light, try to frame the shot with branches, rocks, or other natural features. DSLR, 105mm lens, 1/200 sec, f14, ISO 200.

care not to startle your subject. For those reasons, you will probably want to use a zoom lens. A mid-range telephoto zoom (for example, 70-300mm on a DSLR or 35mm camera) will work for most of the reptiles and mammals you're likely to see Death Valley. If birds are your main interest, there is really no lens that's too long—you will probably want the longest telephoto you can afford.

You may also find that using a tripod slows you down too much, or frightens your subject when you move it. A monopod is a good alternative, giving you much (but not all) of the stability of a tripod while allowing for quicker setup and repositioning. With practice, you can learn to get excellent results using a long lens on a monopod.

Lizards

Lizards are always fun to shoot, whether they are foraging for insects, showing off with a few pushups, or just basking on a rock. Like all reptiles, lizards need to bask in the morning sun to raise their body temperature before starting the day's activities. Lizards are usually easier to approach when they're basking compared to later in the day, when they tend to be more active. During the spring mating season, male lizards can sometimes be approached by imitating their behavior, bobbing your head in response to the pushups they use to announce their presence to females and rival males.

On rocky hillsides and canyons, you're likely to find chuckwallas or collared lizards, two of the larger and more photogenic lizards in the park. When you first see one of these lizards, it has already seen you. It might just be watching, assessing how much of a danger you pose, or it may already be heading for a crevice, or at least toward the other side of the rock. Approach too quickly and it will disappear—but if you're patient, and move slowly and deliberately, you can often get close enough for a good photo. Both species have very good eyesight and depend on having a clear view of their surroundings to avoid predators, so they feel safer when perched on a high rock. With that in mind, approach the lizard from a direction where you won't block its view and the lizard is slightly above you. Think about how you look from the lizard's perspective; you especially don't want to appear as a silhouette against the sky.

Take your time, moving only a few inches with each step, and watch the animal carefully for any sign of stress. If it seems concerned, stop where you are, or back down a little. If a chuckwalla does run into a crevice or other hiding place, find a position about ten feet away and make yourself comfortable. They

Patience has its rewards. When I saw this desert iguana disappear into a burrow, I knew it would come out eventually. I found a good shooting position, far enough away not to frighten the lizard, and waited. When it emerged 30 to 40 minutes later, I was ready for this sequence. 35mm Ektachrome 100VS film, 70-300mm lens at 300mm, ISO 100, exposure data not recorded.

generally don't stay hidden for very long; if you can sit still for 20 or 30 minutes, there's a good chance you'll see it again. I've occasionally seen a chuckwalla disappear behind a rock and then, after I've settled in for a snack, reappear closer to me on another rock. Collared lizards are a different story. In my experience, when you get too close to a collared lizard it will run, and you might not get another chance at it.

Other common lizards include desert iguanas and zebra-tailed lizards, which are often seen among creosote bushes (in other words, almost anywhere in or around Death Valley). Zebra-tailed lizards will sometimes venture out onto the sand dunes, where they can quickly disappear under the surface when threatened. On the Ibex Dunes (p. 90), you might get lucky and see a Mojave fringe-toed lizard, a species that has adapted to living its entire life on the sand. Getting a good shot of a fringe-toed lizard requires a real commitment of time, patience, and sunscreen.

The first time I photographed at Ibex Dunes, I knew I wanted to find a fringe-toed lizard but didn't know much about them. After hiking the dunes for most of a day without seeing so much as a lizard's footprint, I was exhausted and discouraged. In need of a break, I headed for the nearest big creosote bush, collapsed in the broken shade of its skinny branches, and drank the last of my water. That's when I saw it—a fringe-toed lizard, sitting at the edge of the shade about five feet away and eyeing me warily. (You already knew it was there, didn't you?) Since

then I've learned that you rarely see fringe-toes on the open sand; they're usually resting in the partial shade of a creosote. No other lizard has let me sit down next to it like that first one. You need to learn to spot them from a distance, approach slowly—and don't be surprised when they run to the next bush.

Lizards are often out in the harsh light of midday, which can present problems with shadows and contrast. For that reason I always carry a small collapsible reflector in an easily accessible pocket. Have the reflector ready before you approach the lizard. When you get into shooting position, slowly move it to find the angle that will throw some light into the shadows. Be careful, though—too much light will cause the lizard to squint, making your photo look unnatural or just plain weird.

Another way to deal with harsh lighting is to frame the photo with creosote branches, rocks, or whatever else is around. I don't mean you should rearrange the landscape—no lizard I know of would wait around for that. But you can often find a camera position that will place an out-of-focus branch in just the right place to eliminate an otherwise distracting bright spot. Lizards will often rest in the partial shade of a creosote or other shrub, which can create a pleasing dappled lighting effect.

Adding to the challenge of harsh lighting, most lizards are the same color as the rocks or sand they live on. That helps them blend with their surroundings and avoid predators, but it makes life more difficult for wildlife photographers. For more visual separation

Sidewinders make distinctive J-shaped tracks as they move across the sand. 35mm Ektachrome 100VS film, 70-300mm lens at 300mm, ISO 100, exposure data not recorded.

between lizard and background, use a wider aperture to limit depth of field. A too-sharp background can be a distraction that creates confusion in what might otherwise be a good portrait.

Snakes

Snakes are common in Death Valley, but not commonly seen because most species are nocturnal. If you do see a snake, it will probably be in the very early morning or late afternoon. During the day, sidewinders and other rattlesnakes can sometimes be found resting in the shade of creosote bushes (a good reason to watch where you step). Many other snakes spend the daytime in underground burrows and won't be seen at all. Common species in the park include the Panamint rattlesnake, sidewinder (both venomous), Mojave patch-nosed snake, and gopher snake.

While most snakes will avoid you whenever possible, a few species—including at least one rattlesnake—are quite defensive and will stand their ground when they feel threatened. If you aren't familiar with the venomous snakes and how to recognize them, there are some excellent field guides that can help you learn—but until you do, treat all unfamiliar snakes as venomous.

When you find a venomous snake, keep your distance and use a telephoto lens. Always keep one eye on the snake, and be aware of which direction you want to go if it moves toward you. You might be tempted to move in for a close-up, but remember, it may be small and pretty, but it's still potentially deadly—and you're a long way from the nearest hospital.

If you're out on the sand dunes very early and there's little or no wind, you might find some undisturbed tracks of a sidewinder, a mostly nocturnal rattlesnake with a unique method of moving across the dunes. Look for parallel J-shaped tracks in the sand, 10 to 15 inches long and about six inches apart. Try to photograph the tracks the way you would the dunes themselves, with the light coming from the side, to bring out their shape and texture.

Birds

With its diversity of habitats and elevations, Death Valley has more birds than you might expect—the Park Service checklist includes over 300 species. However, many of these are seasonal migrants or occasional visitors, so don't count on finding a large number of bird species in one visit. Birding in Death Valley is a lot like looking for wildflowers; you need to visit several locations to find out what's "in season."

Birds can be found almost anywhere in Death Valley, but if you want a good photo you'll have the most success near springs or other water sources. Bird photography requires patience, careful observation, and the ability to predict where your subject will be. Unlike lizards, birds normally won't let you approach them, and when they fly away they usually don't come back. The best way to photograph birds is to observe their behavior for a while, so you can figure out where you need to be for the shot you want. That might mean sitting quietly near a spring at dawn, or looking for concentrations of insects, seeds, or other food sources. Notice which direction the birds come from, and where they go when they leave, so you can find a shooting position that won't block their route. At the same time, pay attention to the direction of the light and how the background will affect your shot.

When you find a good bird location, it's often best to spend the first day just watching their behavior and making test shots, so you can return the next day at the right time and get into shooting position quickly, disturbing the birds as little as possible. If you find a bird's nest, though, please leave it alone—the adults might be afraid to feed their young or incubate their eggs while you're there. Raptors can be especially sensitive. If you see a hawk's or eagle's nest on a cliff, don't linger too long. You might think you're a safe distance away, but the bird could still be bothered by your presence. (Many

Wilson's warbler, one of the many small bird species that can be found in riparian habitats such as Wildrose Canyon or Darwin Falls. DSLR, 80-400mm lens at 400mm, 1/400 sec, f5.6, ISO 320.

nature magazines no longer publish photos of nesting birds, because they don't want to encourage nest photography.)

Ravens are found throughout the park. They are equally at home scavenging for leftovers around campgrounds and restaurants, hunting lizards and rodents on the sand dunes, or nesting in steep canyons. Golden eagles, the largest birds in the area, inhabit rocky cliffs and might be seen circling high above the canyons and alluvial fans. Closer to the ground, keep an eye out for roadrunners darting from one bush to another as they hunt for snakes and lizards.

One of Death Valley's best birding locations is Saratoga Spring (p. 89), a large lake and marsh at the south end of the park. An important stopover for spring and fall migrants, this oasis sees a high concentration of waterfowl and shorebirds, as well as other marsh birds such as wrens and red-winged blackbirds. Salt Creek Interpretive Trail (p. 65) and Salt Creek Hills (p. 91) are other low-elevation marshes that can be good for bird photography.

Furnace Creek Ranch (p. 77), with its springs, irrigated golf course, palm and tamarisk trees, and other varied habitats, attracts many species of birds that you might not find in other locations. Similarly, the buildings around Stovepipe Wells Village (p. 61) and the picnic area at Scotty's Castle (p. 57) also attract a variety of birds.

The springs in Wildrose Canyon (p. 100), above and below the campground, are good places to look for warblers, finches, and orioles, as well as chukars and quail on the nearby hillsides. Farther up the canyon, toward Wildrose Peak (p. 102) and Telescope Peak (p. 103), you might find grosbeaks or other species common to this piñon-juniper habitat. Other birding spots for the adventurous (with four-wheel-drive vehicles) include the upper reaches of Hanaupah Canyon (p. 92) and Warm Spring Canyon (p. 93).

Amphibians and fish

Amphibians and fish? In Death Valley?

The prehistoric lake that once covered Death Valley was home to many species of fish, including a two-inch member of the Cyprinodont family called the pupfish. Pupfish are remarkably tolerant of extremes of temperature and salinity. As the climate changed and the formerly temperate lake was reduced to a small number of hot, salty ponds, they were the only survivors. Because the remaining water sources were unconnected to each other, the ancestral fish evolved into a number of distinct species. Today there are several isolated populations of pupfish in the valley. Saratoga Spring (p. 89) and Salt Creek (p. 65) each has its own unique, endemic species.

Pupfish breed in shallow water, only a couple inches deep. When a male finds a good spot for a nest he will try to entice a female to lay her eggs there, while at the same time defending the site from other males. Photographing this behavior, or just getting a good shot of a fish, can be tricky. If you have a telephoto lens with close focusing abilities, or one with a macro mode, you will definitely need it here. If not, you'll probably want to crop the photo when you get home.

Pupfish are sensitive to your movements, and there are very few places you can approach them close enough for a good photo. The best place I can suggest to shoot pupfish is from the boardwalk at Salt Creek. Walk the length of the boardwalk and find an area where the pupfish are active and you're able to get relatively close. (Stay on the boardwalk—the habitat here is very sensitive, and besides, if you step off you could find yourself stuck in the mud.) To minimize reflec-

Male (left) and female pupfish, photographed from the boardwalk at the Salt Creek Interpretive Trail. DSLR, 70-300mm lens at 200mm, 1/500 sec, f9, ISO 100.

Flame skimmer, a large dragonfly common along the creek below Darwin Falls. Dragonflies will often return to the same perch several times in a few minutes. When you see one, stop and watch its behavior. Getting a good shot might be easier than you expect. A fast shutter speed helps to freeze its motion, while a wider aperture reduces depth of field, eliminating distractions from the background. DSLR, 300mm lens, 1/1000 sec, f4.5, ISO 200.

will likely be scared away while you are getting into position. Once you're ready, relax and wait a while. If the fish haven't returned in 15 minutes, you're too close and should move to another spot.

Death Valley's amphibians are few and far between—they can't tolerate high salinity the way pupfish can—but they do exist. I have occasionally found tadpoles of western toads in the creek below Darwin Falls (p. 106). Photographing them is very similar to working with pupfish, only harder. Breeding pupfish have a strong incentive to return to their chosen spot, but the tadpoles seem to be happy anywhere in the creek, so if you scare them away they might not come back. There are also isolated populations of treefrogs in the park, including one in the upper part of Hanaupah Canyon (p. 92). Finding a frog or toad in the desert is always a treat—a reminder of the diversity of life here, and its ability to survive and adapt even in the harshest conditions.

Insects and spiders

In addition to its many lizards, you will soon discover that Death Valley has an abundant and varied invertebrate population. (All those lizards have to eat something!) The variety seems endless: tarantulas and other spiders; scorpions; butterflies, moths, and their caterpillars; cactus bees … a photographer specializing in entomology could spend a lifetime here and never run out of subject matter.

The cactus bees are my favorite. In spring,

tions off the water, position yourself so the sun is behind you and slightly to your side. A polarizing filter will help to reduce reflections and make the colors of the fish appear brighter. Make sure you are not casting a shadow on the water; the fish won't like it, and it will ruin your photo anyway. The fish when the beavertails and other cactus are in bloom, you'll find these bees "swimming" deep into the flowers, often so covered in pollen that you won't even see them at first.

Shooting these little critters requires some specialized equipment. Fortunately, there is plenty to choose from—but you may not feel so fortunate when you see the price of some of that equipment. I've seen many different approaches to insect photography, depending on just how close you want to get and what kind of lighting you like to use.

The first thing you'll need is a lens that is capable of focusing at close distances (usually called a macro lens, or occasionally a micro lens). Personally, I like to use a 105mm macro lens on my DSLR. The focal length provides a good working distance, allowing me to get close enough to get the shot while leaving enough room between lens and subject so the lens doesn't block my light.

Next you'll need a flash, or two or three; it's rarely possible to do insect photography using only available light. My preference is to use one flash with a diffuser—either a miniature softbox that attaches directly to the flash, or a slightly larger one that mounts on a bracket. I rarely have the flash mounted directly on the camera. Instead, I either attach it to a bracket that extends beside and slightly above the camera, or I hold the flash in my left hand while holding the camera in my right.

I know many photographers who prefer to use two flashes for insects and other small subjects, and in some situations I do the same. Using a bracket that holds both

A pair of gray snout beetles mating on a branch of a creosote bush at the Mesquite Flat Sand Dunes. DSLR, 105mm lens, 1/200 sec, f9, ISO 100.

flashes, you can position your lights on either side of the lens and adjust them individually, perhaps with one slightly higher and/or brighter than the other, to create the desired lighting effect.

There are entire close-up systems available, with brackets, flashes, cables, power packs, miniature reflectors, and diffusers, all designed to give you complete control of your close-up photography—and to separate you from your cash. Before investing in one of these systems, experiment a little and see if you can get what you want with a simpler, less expensive setup.

I usually choose a single flash, hand held, because it allows me to react quickly to a moving subject. As with other animals, I want an insect's head to be toward the light

Mojave fringe-toed lizard on the Ibex Dunes. This composition shows a close-up of the lizard, and at the same time places it in the surrounding habitat—a perspective that's possible only if you get down on the ground and meet the animal in its own world. 35mm Ektachrome Lumiere 100 film, 200mm lens, ISO 100, exposure data not recorded.

(unless I'm deliberately emphasizing another feature), so I need to move the flash when the bug changes direction, something that's harder to do with a bracket-mounted flash. At close distances, a small, on-flash diffuser is all it takes to soften the light and avoid harsh shadows.

Mammals

The most common mammals you'll see in Death Valley are the rabbits—both jackrabbits and cottontails. Jackrabbits are often seen out in the open and are distinguished by their huge ears and long legs, while cottontails are shyer, smaller, more rounded, and have fluffy white tails. They're both challenging to photograph. When you see a jackrabbit it's usually running full speed away from you, and your typical view of a cottontail is its fluffy white tail disappear-

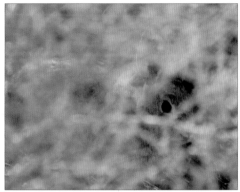

ing behind a nearby creosote bush or into a burrow.

As with other wildlife, long lenses and patience are the key. If you see a rabbit and it's not already running away from you, stop for a few minutes. Take some time to observe its behavior, to figure out what it's doing and where it might go next. At the same time, the rabbit will be observing you, getting accustomed to your presence, and hopefully learning that you're not a threat. Don't act like a predator; that is, don't focus your attention only on the rabbit. Look around, always keeping one eye on your prey but appearing to be interested in something else. You may not be close enough for a photo at this point, but after a few minutes you should be able to get a little closer. Maybe. If the rabbit is in the right mood.

Coyotes are another common mammal in the park, and whether you get a photo seems entirely up to them. I once watched a coyote playing with a branch on the lawn at Scotty's Castle for a half hour; it seemed completely unconcerned about my presence. Other times, a coyote has seen me from a quarter mile away and promptly headed

Rabbits are abundant in Death Valley. Cottontails are smaller, rounder, and, as their name implies, have fluffy white tails. You're most likely to see them in the early evening, just as the sun is going down. Jackrabbits are larger, with long legs and huge ears, and can be seen at any time of day. Both species can be shy when it comes to being photographed. Jackrabbits usually run away at full speed, while cottontails will often hide behind a bush. Top: Cottontail at sunset. DSLR, 70-300mm lens at 300mm, 1/320 sec, f8, ISO 200. Middle: Cottontail behind bush. DSLR, 80-400mm lens at 400mm, 1/400 sec, f5.6, ISO 100. Bottom: Jackrabbit. DSLR, 80-400mm lens at 270mm, 1/400 sec, f5.3, ISO 180.

Coyotes will occasionally tolerate photographers at close range. This one was in the picnic area at Scotty's Castle. 35mm Ektachrome 100VS film, 70-300mm lens, ISO 100, focal length and exposure data not recorded.

Roadrunners are symbolic of the desert. You can often see them around the shops and other buildings at Furnace Creek. DSLR, 300mm lens, 1/400 sec, f6.3, ISO 200.

in the opposite direction. You're likely to get your best photos of coyotes from your car—they seem to feel far less threatened by cars than by people on foot. If you see a coyote walking along the road, drive past it and find a safe place to pull over, so you can get into position and let it come to you. It won't always work out—sometimes the coyote will change direction and head away from you—but your patience might be rewarded with a great portrait.

Less common mammals in the park include bighorn sheep and mountain lions—if you see one of these, consider yourself lucky!

The cat that waited for me

One of my most memorable experiences with Death Valley wildlife happened one afternoon in Wildrose Canyon. I had arrived at the campground at about 5:00 and, after a long day of driving, was eager to stretch my legs and have a look around. I started down the trail that leads past a small spring, thick with mesquite, at the far end of the campground. Almost immediately, I saw a bobcat on the hillside, just above my eye level and no more than ten steps in front of me. I stopped. It stopped. I took a step back; it took a step back. Neither of us knew what to do next. It was so close, and so unexpected, that I needed a few seconds to really understand what it was. I ran through a checklist in my mind: tufted ears ... short tail ... long legs ... spots ... twice as tall as a house cat ... this was definitely a bobcat.

Have I mentioned that my camera was still in the car, a hundred yards behind me?

For the next few seconds, while the cat and I stared at each other, I had two conflicting impulses. The first, of course, was to run back for my camera. The other was to stay where I was and enjoy the moment—I had never been this close to a bobcat before and might never be again. And besides, did I really expect a bobcat to just sit and wait for me? I decided to go for the camera. All the way to the car, and all the way back, I cursed myself. How could I be so stupid as to walk away from my camera in a place like Wildrose? I knew I'd never see the cat again, at least not that close.

I guessed the cat would go up the hill, so on the way back I went up the hill myself, coming over a low ridge a few yards above where it had been. I stood for a while, scanning the hillside as well as the trail and spring below. Nothing. Then I thought I saw movement behind a small shrub about 20 feet below me. Something was different about that bush; the ground behind it was the wrong shade of brown. I aimed my lens at the bush, trying to focus beyond the branches on whatever might be behind them. When the cat's face popped into focus I couldn't believe what I was seeing. Yes, the bobcat had sat—literally—right where I had left it, and waited for me to return with my camera. Thank you, Mother Nature!

I moved left for a better view. The cat looked at me for a moment, then walked downhill toward the spring—and lay down in the shade of another bush. A minute later, it stood up and disappeared into the mesquite.

I stayed for two days and never saw the cat again. I had three photos, and one more surprise from Death Valley.

A female Brewer's blackbird perches in a creosote bush near Ubehebe Crater. The first light of sunrise warms the colors of both the bird and the leaves, and provides interesting sidelighting. DSLR, 300mm lens, 1/1000 sec, f4.5, ISO 200.

Sidewinders are nearly always found on the ground; I've only seen climbing behavior twice. When this one climbed into a small shrub, I took advantage of the opportunity for an unusual shot of its shadow. DSLR, 105mm lens, 1/125 sec, f25, ISO 200.

Death Valley National Park

to Big Pine

Eureka Dunes

Scotty's Castle

Grapevine Ranger Station

Beatty

NORTH
page 53

EAST/CENTRAL
page 61

to Las Vegas

The Racetrack

Stovepipe Wells Village

Lone Pine

WEST
page 97

Emigrant

Furnace Creek

Zabriskie Point

Panamint Springs

Wildrose

Badwater

Dante's View

SOUTH
page 75

Shoshone

California

to Baker

Ridgecrest

North

0 2   10   20 Kilometers
0 2   10   20 Miles

Location Listings

Here's the part you've been waiting for, the real details about where to go and what to shoot.

The locations are divided into four general areas. Within each area, specific sites are listed in order of their geographic location. Some locations don't fit neatly into the list, so make sure you check your map before driving from one to the next.

Since I can't know which direction you're coming from, the directions to each location start at the nearest major landmark, such as Stovepipe Wells Village or Grapevine Ranger Station. Before starting out, you'll want to see where you are on your map and adjust the directions accordingly.

Remember that road conditions can change drastically from one year to the next, or even from season to season, so you should check the latest conditions before driving on any unpaved road. The Death Valley Morning Report, posted at ranger stations and other locations throughout the park as well as online, lists road closures and other conditions.

Each location includes the dates when wildflowers might be in bloom in a typical year. That doesn't mean you'll always find flowers, or that the bloom will last for the entire time period. But in most years, if there are flowers, you'll probably find them blooming in the months I've indicated.

The approximate elevation is included for each location, which can be helpful in looking for wildflowers as well as predicting the temperature. The chart on pp. 8–9 shows the average temperatures at Furnace Creek, which is near sea level. At other locations, the temperature will be lower by about 3 to 5° F for each 1,000 feet of elevation.

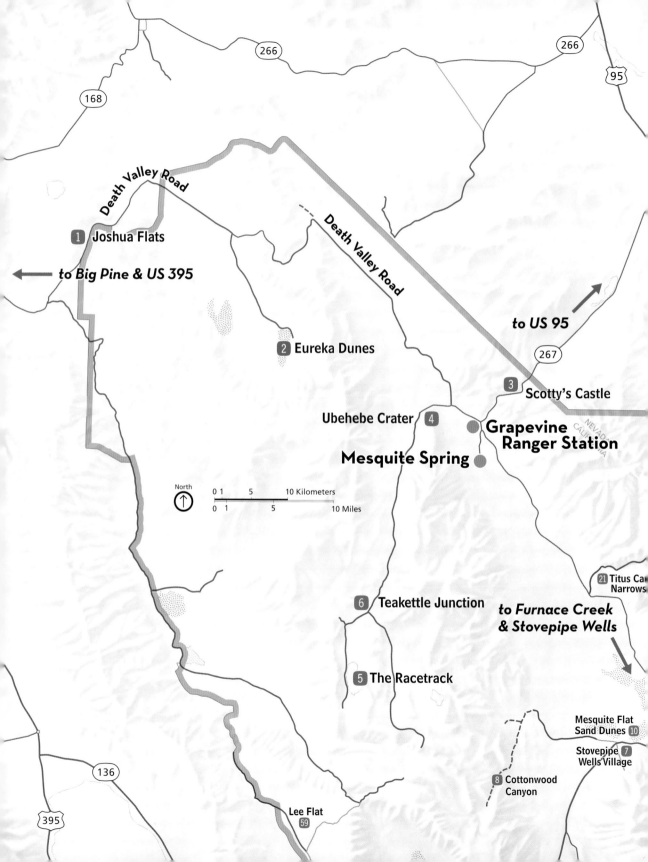

266

266

95

168

Death Valley Road

Death Valley Road

1 Joshua Flats

← to Big Pine & US 395

2 Eureka Dunes

to US 95

267

3 Scotty's Castle

Ubehebe Crater 4

Grapevine
Ranger Station

Mesquite Spring

NEVADA
CALIFORNIA

North
↑

0 1   5   10 Kilometers

0 1   5   10 Miles

21 Titus Ca
Narrows

6 Teakettle Junction

to Furnace Creek
& Stovepipe Wells

5 The Racetrack

Mesquite Flat
Sand Dunes 10

Stovepipe 7
Wells Village

136

8 Cottonwood
Canyon

395

Lee Flat
59

North

The northern section of the park is the least developed, with few paved roads and fewer facilities. The nearest gas stations, restaurants, and lodging are in Big Pine (on US 395 northwest of the park) and Stovepipe Wells Village. Camping is available at Mesquite Spring and Eureka Dunes. Restrooms or pit toilets can be found at the campgrounds as well as at Grapevine Ranger Station and Scotty's Castle.

1 Joshua Flats

Highlights: Joshua trees, reptiles
Flowers: April–May
Best light: Early morning, late afternoon
Elevation: 6,100'
Access: Paved road from Big Pine; mostly gravel roads between Joshua Flats and Death Valley

Joshua Flats, at the northern boundary of the park, is my favorite place to photograph Joshua trees. 35mm Ektachrome 100S film, ISO 100, lens and exposure data not recorded.

One of the larger Joshua tree forests in the area, this is by far my favorite. I've often stopped here for a couple hours of shooting on the way in or out of Death Valley. The combination of blue sky, white clouds, and the odd, twisted shapes of Joshua trees can contribute to some dramatic compositions, and the choice of east- or west-facing slopes assures good light in morning or afternoon.

Driving toward Death Valley from Big Pine, the abrupt transition from piñon-juniper woodland to Joshua tree forest makes these bizarrely shaped yuccas seem even more unusual. It's pretty good going the other direction, too, as the view changes from creosotes to Joshuas at the southern end of the forest.

The road passes through Joshua trees for about five miles, with the densest stands in a gently sloping valley. There are no marked viewpoints or turnouts here; just find an area with good light and look for a wide spot in the road to park your car.

At this elevation, winter snowstorms are not uncommon. If you're lucky enough to be here on a clear day after it snows, you'll get some fantastic photos.

Directions: From Big Pine, E on SR168

for 2.5 miles; turn right onto Death Valley Road (called Big Pine Road on some maps) for 19 to 24 miles, stopping wherever you like. From Grapevine Ranger Station, NW toward Ubehebe Crater for 2.8 miles; turn right onto unpaved Death Valley Road (Big Pine Road) for 47 to 52 miles.

2 Eureka Dunes

Highlights: Sand dunes, reptiles, rare flowers
Flowers: March–April
Best light: Early morning, late afternoon
Elevation: 3,500'
Access: Up to 40 miles of gravel roads; sandy dirt roads near the dunes

Located in Eureka Valley between the Saline Range and Last Chance Range, the Eureka Dunes are California's tallest, rising more than 680 feet above the valley floor. Towering over the dunes, the gray, pink, and black strata of the Last Chance Range make this a strong setting for landscape photography. The most dramatic lighting will occur in the morning, when the dunes are in sunlight and the face of the mountain is still in shadow, and late afternoon, when the setting sun warms the color of both the dunes and the mountains.

These dunes receive more rainfall than other dunes in the area, because of their location at the base of a west-facing steep mountain range, and they are isolated from other sandy areas. For those reasons, three endemic (that is, living here and nowhere else) species of plants have evolved here: Eureka

Above: Scotty's Castle provides an abundance of architectural details to focus on. DSLR, 80-200mm lens at 185mm, 1/25 sec, f16, ISO 200.   **Below:** Scotty's Castle, a monument to Death Valley's greatest con man. DSLR, 80-200mm lens at 86mm, 1/40 sec, f16, ISO 200.

Walking to the bottom of Ubehebe Crater is easy,
but getting back up can be a long, slow hike. DSLR,
18-70mm lens at 18mm, 1/200 sec, f10, ISO 100.

Dunes evening primrose, a large white flower that blooms at night and is pollinated by moths; Eureka dunegrass, a tough grass that grows higher on the dunes than any other plant; and shining milkvetch, a silvery plant that grows in hummocks like the dunegrass. There are also five endemic species of beetles living on the dunes.

To photograph dune plants, be prepared to get down on your belly and find an interesting background; you'll have plenty of choices. The primrose and dunegrass are federally listed endangered species, and the milkvetch is a candidate for listing, so be careful not to do any damage when you photograph them. (This advice applies equally to all plants, animals, rocks, historic and prehistoric sites, and everything else in the park.)

As you hike on these dunes, you may hear a deep rumbling sound that seems to come from everywhere at once. It's been compared to the deepest bass note of a pipe organ.

Looking up from the inside of Ubehebe Crater.
DSLR, 300mm lens, 1/500 sec, f7.1, ISO 200.

You're not hallucinating! The exact mechanism isn't fully understood, but the sound is caused by the sand shifting as you walk on it. If there's too much moisture in the sand—a common condition in winter and spring—no sound will be produced.

Hiking east of the dunes, you'll find several steep canyons to explore. Just be sure you carry water and allow plenty of extra time; the distances here can be deceiving.

Directions: From Big Pine, E on SR168 for 2.5 miles; turn right onto Death Valley Road (called Big Pine Road on some maps) for about 40 miles; turn right on South Eureka Road for 11 miles. Pavement ends about 35 miles from Big Pine. From Grapevine Ranger Station, NW toward Ubehebe Crater for 2.8 miles; turn right onto unpaved Death Valley Road (Big Pine Road) for 33 miles; turn left on South Eureka Road for 11 miles.

Caution: Park only in the designated parking area, to avoid getting stuck in the sand.

③ Scotty's Castle

Highlights: History, architecture, birds
Flowers: March–April
Best light: Late afternoon, but not too late
Elevation: 3,000'
Access: Paved road; guided tours

In the 1920s prospector and con man Walter Scott, a.k.a. Death Valley Scotty, told everyone this elaborate Spanish-style mansion was built with the fortune he made from his secret gold mine. In fact, it was owned by Albert and Bessie Johnson, millionaires from Chicago. Originally recruited as inves-

The Racetrack is not easy to get to, but you'll be rewarded with dramatic landscapes. 35mm Ektachrome 100S film, ISO 100, lens and exposure data not recorded.

tors in Scotty's fictional mine, the Johnsons fell in love with the location and decided to build their vacation home here. Their friendship—and cash—allowed Scotty to continue his flamboyant lifestyle. The guided tours available here are a fun way to learn some of the colorful history of Death Valley.

The "castle" actually consists of several buildings, any of which can be an attractive photo subject, with an abundance of interesting architectural details, mosaics, and lavish furnishings. Be sure to ask a ranger whether it's OK to use a tripod or a flash inside; the answer may depend on how many other people are visiting that day. Around the grounds, you'll find a variety of bird species, attracted by the riparian habitat of Grapevine Canyon.

Scotty's Castle has great light in late afternoon, but because of its canyon location it could be in shadow an hour or more before sunset. Make sure you arrive early enough to catch the light.

Directions: From Grapevine Ranger Station, follow the signs to Scotty's Castle, about 3 miles NE.

④ Ubehebe Crater

Highlights: Volcanic craters; hiking
Flowers: Not likely
Best light: Early morning, late afternoon
Elevation: 2,500'
Access: Paved road; moderate 1.5-mile
walk around the rim; easy hike to the
bottom of the crater; difficult hike
back to the top

Ubehebe Crater, half a mile across and 600 feet deep, is the largest of several volcanic craters in this area, each of them created when rising magma reached groundwater and turned it instantly to steam, resulting in a powerful explosion. The craters and surrounding cinder fields are a landscape unlike anything else you'll find in Death Valley. Follow the trail around Ubehebe's rim for views of the cinder fields and some of the smaller craters.

One of the best views of Ubehebe, conveniently, is from the parking lot, where you can see the crater's colorful eastern wall. Late afternoon light will bring out the colors in this cutaway view of the alluvial fan that was blasted away by the eruption. On the other hand, getting up early to watch the sun rise over the crater can also be rewarding. Then if you hike down the trail toward the bottom you can watch it rise again and again. Just remember, it's a lot harder hiking back up.

At the bottom of the crater is a miniature mud playa, where the concentration of water has allowed creosote bushes to reach heights of ten feet or more. Unfortunately the mud is not as photogenic here as on more remote playas, because the mosaic patterns are broken up by footprints. Standing inside the crater, looking up at the rim, you really start to appreciate how big it is, and how much force was required to create it. You can make yourself dizzy spinning around trying to take it all in. Walking back up, take the northern branch of the trail, to your right. It's a little longer, but a much easier climb.

Directions: From Grapevine Ranger Station, follow the signs to Ubehebe Crater, about 6 miles NW.

⑤ The Racetrack
⑥ Teakettle Junction

Highlights: Mysterious moving rocks,
huge dry lakebed
Flowers: March–April
Best light: Early morning, late afternoon
Elevation: Racetrack 3,700', Teakettle
Junction 4,200'

**Access: Unpaved road, rough in spots;
   high clearance needed**

The Racetrack is famous for its "skating rocks" and the trails they make as they slide across the mud playa when the rain and wind conditions are just right. The best rock trails will be found in the southeast corner of the playa, a couple miles south of the parking area.

Almost any photo you make here will show the weirdness of rocks moving across the desert. The challenge is finding a composition that will be creative and artistic as well. I like to use a wide-angle lens, exaggerating the rock's size with an apparently endless trail behind it. Or just the opposite—put the trail in the foreground with the rock disappearing in the distance. Take some time and find a composition that speaks to you. Whatever you do, DO NOT move the rocks! They're amazing enough where they are, so don't try to improve them.

Even without the skating rocks, Racetrack Playa is a wonderful place for photography, whether you're shooting grand landscapes or detailed close-ups. The mosaic of the playa's surface contains patterns within patterns that can keep you busy for hours. The Grandstand, a large black rock outcrop near the north end of the playa, stands in stark contrast to the rest of the scenery and offers a great view of the playa as well as habitat for lizards and wildflowers.

The road to the Racetrack can be very rough, rattling your car as well as your nerves for at least an hour each way. Once as I was driving back from a day of shooting I noticed a piece of someone's bumper

Creosote bush at dusk. 35mm Ektachrome Lumiere 100X film, 20mm lens, ISO 100, exposure data not recorded.

in the road. At my next stop I discovered it was mine; it had fallen off on my way out that morning.

On the way to the Racetrack, you'll probably want to stop for a photo at Teakettle Junction, an unexpected bit of whimsy along the way. If you have an extra teakettle, feel free to add it to the collection!

Directions: From Grapevine Ranger Station, follow the signs to Ubehebe Crater, about 6 miles NW; then S on Racetrack Valley Road about 27 miles (the turnoff is before you reach the Ubehebe parking lot).

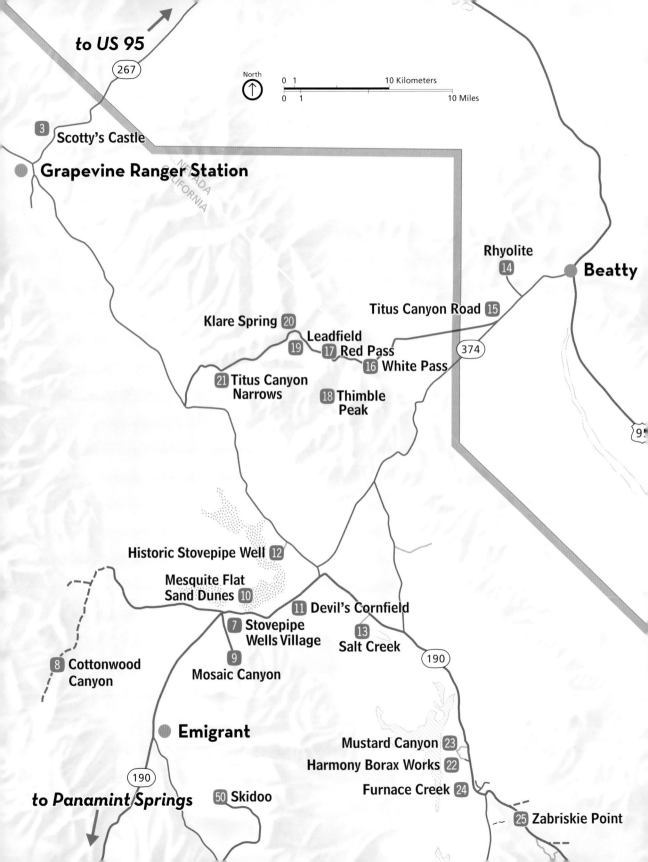

East/Central

Most of the locations in this section are accessible to passenger cars, via paved roads or short dirt roads. Gas stations, restaurants, lodging, and restrooms can be found at Stovepipe Wells Village and in Beatty, Nevada. Campgrounds are located at Stovepipe Wells Village and Emigrant.

7 Stovepipe Wells Village

Highlights: Birds, history; also food, gas, and lodging
Flowers: February–March
Best light: Early morning
Elevation: Sea level
Access: Paved road

You might not think of Stovepipe Wells Village as a location for photography. For most people it's just a place to stop for gas or lunch. Others make the motel or campground their home base while they spend the days visiting other locations around the park. Campers often take advantage of the showers at the swimming pool, which are available for a reasonable fee.

But there are things to see and photograph here as well. Around the motel and general store you'll find several historic items, including wagon wheels, ore cars, and wagons. The many tamarisks and other shade trees, as well as the various water sources, attract a variety of bird life. Spend some time sitting on a bench in the shade and you might get a shot of a curious raven or roadrunner.

Directions: SR190 near the center of the park.

8 Cottonwood Canyon

Highlights: Canyon views, off-trail hiking
Flowers: April–May
Best light: Early morning
Elevation: 2,000'
Access: 12 to 18 miles of sandy dirt road; 4WD needed

The road to Cottonwood Canyon starts near sea level, passing through creosote bush scrub and gradually climbing to about 2,000 feet. The lower part of the road is a good place to look for wildlife, including desert iguanas, roadrunners, and sidewinders. In warm weather, snakes will usually be out very early, while the lizards will be active a little later in the day.

As the road ascends into the Cottonwood Mountains you'll notice a change in habitat, with chuckwallas and spiny lizards sharing the rocky hillsides with rock nettle and prickly poppy. About 11 miles from the highway, the road forks, with Marble Canyon to the right and Cottonwood to the left.

Cottonwood is not as steep or narrow as some of Death Valley's other canyons. In many places you can hike up the side of the canyon for some good views of the surrounding mountains as well as views of Death Valley.

Directions: Just W of Stovepipe Wells Village, turn N toward the campground for 0.1 mile, then left toward the airport; at about 0.5 mile the airstrip is on your left; continue

An approaching storm stirs up the sand dunes at Mesquite Flat. 35mm Ektachrome 100VS film, 70-300mm lens, ISO 100, focal length and exposure data not recorded.

to the right for 12 to 18 miles. Caution: Requires four-wheel drive and experience driving in sand.

9 Mosaic Canyon

Highlights: Patterns in canyon walls, hiking
Flowers: February–March
Best light: It's complicated
Elevation: 1,000'

Access: 2.5-mile gravel road; mostly easy 3.5-mile hike (round trip) with occasional rock scrambling

This is a beautiful little canyon, with polished marble, intricate mosaic patterns, and other geologic attractions. The best marble is found about ¼ mile from the parking area, where the canyon becomes very narrow. Here you'll find an endless variety of patterns in the marble and breccia of the canyon walls, polished smooth by centuries of flash floods.

Because of the canyon's narrowness and orientation, you might not get the light you want in the early morning or late afternoon,

Ripples in the sand dunes at Mesquite Flat. Backlighting adds contrast and makes the sand appear to sparkle. 35mm Ektachrome 100VS film, ISO 100, lens and exposure data not recorded.

which means you'll probably be photographing the marble in the harsher light of midday. In that light, the colors of the rock can seem faded or washed out. Here's a trick to bring out the color in a close-up: Pour a little water on the rock and spread it around so it's evenly distributed. At first the rock will just look wet and the colors unnatural. But as the water starts to evaporate there will be a moment when the rock appears dry, while the colors are still enhanced. That's when to make your shot.

Above the narrows, the marble gives way to high rock walls in all shades of red. Because the canyon is wider here, you're more likely to find good light in early morning (on the east-facing walls) and late afternoon (on the west-facing walls).

Directions: About ¼ mile W of Stovepipe Wells Village, turn S off the highway onto Mosaic Canyon Road for about 2.5 miles.

⑩ Mesquite Flat Sand Dunes

Highlights: Sand dunes, reptiles, insects,
  hiking
Flowers: February–March
Best light: Early morning, late afternoon
Elevation: Sea level
Access: Paved road; easy walk out to the
  dunes

These are the most accessible, and most visited, sand dunes in Death Valley—but that doesn't necessarily mean they're crowded. Most people only walk a couple hundred feet from the parking lot. If you're willing to walk a little farther, you'll be rewarded with sweeping views, dramatic photos, and maybe even a little solitude.

The best light is in late afternoon, when the low angle of the sun emphasizes the shadows and textures, while early morning is best if you're looking for animal tracks and fewer human footprints. In and around the creosote bushes, look for desert iguanas, zebra-tailed lizards, and a comical-looking, inch-long critter called a gray snout beetle.

For a more unusual view, hike out after dark with a tripod and shoot the dunes in moonlight. Just remember that sidewinders are nocturnal; bring a flashlight and watch where you step.

Directions: 2 miles E of Stovepipe Wells Village on SR190.

⑪ Devil's Cornfield

Highlights: Unusual vegetation, reptiles
Flowers: February–March
Best light: Early morning, late afternoon
Elevation: Sea level
Access: Paved road

It's not corn but arrowweed, growing in odd-looking hummocks, that inspired the name of this spot. Between the shrubs, depending on the time of year, you might find annual grasses, a few wildflowers, or just dry sandy ground. Look closely at the saltgrass to find the salt crystals that are left behind as moisture evaporates from its leaves.

North of the road, you should have good light in both early morning and late afternoon; you'll also see more footprints, as it appears that most people prefer to explore in this direction. Walk at least a few yards off the path for a better photo, especially if you want to shoot the mosaic patterns in the dried mud. Walk a little farther to the west and you can use the Mesquite Flat Sand Dunes as a background for an early morning photo.

South of the road, the light is best in the early morning, with Tucki Mountain providing the backdrop for dramatic landscapes.

Directions: 5 miles E of Stovepipe Wells Village on SR190.

⑫ Historic Stovepipe Well

Highlights: History, reptiles
Flowers: February–March
Best light: Early morning, late afternoon

The original well that gave Stovepipe Wells its name. A length of stovepipe was placed on the pump to make it easier to find in drifting sand. DSLR, 10-24mm lens at 20mm, 1/200 sec, f13, ISO 200.

Elevation: Sea level
Access: 1-mile dirt road

It may not be much to look at, but this iron pump on the edge of the sand dunes could have saved your life if you were crossing here in 1905. The only water source in this part of the valley, the pump was often obscured by shifting sand, so a length of stovepipe was inserted to make it easier to find. The well itself has been covered with concrete for safety, and the pump handle has been removed, but the rest of the pump is still here.

This spot also provides an alternative access to the Mesquite Flat Sand Dunes—hike toward the southwest—and is a good location for lizard photography.

About halfway along the dirt road to the well is the grave of Val Nolan, about whom very little is known. It's said that he was last seen alive at Beatty in July 1931, but there's no record of who he was. His body was found and buried here by a movie company in November 1931.

Directions: From Stovepipe Wells Village, E on SR190 about 7 miles; turn left toward Scotty's Castle for about 3 miles. The unmarked turnoff will be on your left; drive about a mile to the end of the dirt road.

13 Salt Creek Interpretive Trail

Highlights: Birds, pupfish, salt marsh
Flowers: February–March
Best light: Early morning, late afternoon
Elevation: -200'
Access: 1-mile dirt road; ½-mile
    boardwalk

The wooden boardwalk makes this an easy (and wheelchair accessible) location to shoot while protecting this very delicate marsh habitat from the damage caused by foot traffic. The boardwalk takes you through otherwise inaccessible areas that are thick with pickleweed and other marsh plants. Other parts of the creek are more open, where you can photograph the surrounding badlands reflected in the water.

In spring, you can photograph the pupfish that live here. Find a spot where you have a good view of shallow water, sit quietly at the edge of the boardwalk, and watch the bright blue males as they defend their potential nesting sites from each other and attempt to impress the females. Use a telephoto lens, preferably one with macro-focusing capabilities, so you won't get too close and scare them away. A polarizing filter will help to limit reflections from the water. (See p. 43 for more about photographing pupfish.)

Depending on the season, you'll also find a variety of birds here, feeding on the abundant insects, as well as the usual assortment of lizards and occasional snakes. I once saw a sidewinder resting in the shade of the boardwalk—one more reminder to watch where you put your hands and feet.

Directions: From Stovepipe Wells Village, E on SR190 about 11.5 miles. The turnout will be on your right.

14 Rhyolite, Bottle House, and Goldwell Open Air Museum

Highlights: Ghost town, outdoor
    sculptures
Flowers: April–May
Best light: Early morning,
    late afternoon
Elevation: 3,800'
Access: Paved road

The ruins of Rhyolite's banks, brothels, and

In Rhyolite, the ruins of the Porter Brothers general store, as seen through the windows of the school. DSLR, 70-300mm lens at 80mm, 1/30 sec, f22, ISO 100.

other buildings provide endless photo opportunities. Take some time to wander among the ruins and shoot whatever appeals to you. Try shooting from different perspectives, or using the ruins of one building to frame a shot of another. The weathered wood of the smaller buildings holds unexpected details of texture and color.

Dramatic compositions can be found here any time of day, although, as with most subjects, you'll have the best light in early morning or late afternoon. At sunrise the warm light on the Amargosa Desert can make a dramatic background for the ruins when you're shooting from the upper end of town. This can also be an interesting location for nighttime photography, using flash or moonlight.

The larger concrete buildings are located along the paved road. The jail and many smaller wooden buildings are scattered on dirt roads to the east of the paved road. You can drive into that area, but I recommend walking; you'll see more that way and probably make better photos.

At the lower end of town are the Goldwell Open Air Museum, with its large outdoor sculptures, and the Bottle House, built by miner Tom Kelly from 50,000 beer and liquor bottles.

See p. 30 for more information about Rhyolite.

Directions: From Stovepipe Wells Village,

E on SR190 about 7 miles; turn left toward Scotty's Castle for about 0.6 mile; right for another 22 miles; left at the sign for Rhyolite. From Beatty, Nevada, W on SR374 about 4 miles; turn right at the sign for Rhyolite.

15 Titus Canyon Road

Highlights: See locations 16–21
Access: 25-mile one-way dirt road; rough
in spots; narrow, with steep cliffs

The Park Service web site says you need two to three hours to drive Titus Canyon Road, but whoever wrote that was obviously not a photographer. Plan on anywhere between six hours and a full day—last time I was there, I started the drive before 6 AM and finally emerged from the mouth of the canyon sometime after 5 PM.

Driving is easier and safer—and you'll have better light—if you start early in the morning, with the sun behind you, rather than later in the day, when it's shining directly into your windshield. This is a 25-mile one-way road, so once you get started you're committed to it for a while.

After crossing the Amargosa Desert, with its abundant creosote bush, cactus, and other lower-elevation plants, the road climbs into the Grapevine Mountains for some spectacular, sweeping views before descending into what is probably the steepest, narrowest canyon you've ever driven through. This is one drive where you might wish you had brought a geologist along to explain what you're seeing. A good alternative is *Geology of Death Valley National Park*, by Miller and Wright,

Walking on the Mesquite Flat dunes at sunrise, I held the camera at waist level for this shot of my shadow on the sand. Since I couldn't see exactly what I was shooting, it took several tries to get the right composition. DSLR, 18-70mm lens at 18mm, 1/20 sec, f22, ISO 100.

for sale at the Furnace Creek Visitor Center. It includes a mile-by-mile description of Titus Canyon geology.

There are no facilities of any kind along this road, although when you finish the drive you'll find restrooms next to the parking area. To get an early start, I recommend spending the previous night in Beatty, Nevada (6 miles east), where you can find several motels, restaurants, and gas stations. Stovepipe Wells Village (27 miles west) has a campground as well as food, gas, and motel rooms.

Directions: From Stovepipe Wells Village, E on SR190 about 7 miles; turn left toward Scotty's Castle for about 0.6 mile; then right for another 20 miles; the turnoff will be on your left, marked by a small sign. From Beatty, Nevada, W on SR374 about 6 miles; turn right at the sign for Titus Canyon. The beginning of Titus Canyon Road can be a little confusing, because the road seems to split off in different directions—but the forks reconnect after a hundred yards or so. As long as you're heading west, you should be OK.

Caution: Do NOT attempt to drive this road in the rain, in any vehicle. Beyond White Pass the road can be very slippery, and you could end up at the bottom of a cliff. The narrow parts of the canyon are subject to flash flooding. The road is sometimes closed by washouts, mud, or snow, and may be closed in summer because of extreme heat. Be sure to check the current road conditions before starting this drive.

16 White Pass

Mile 9.6, Titus Canyon Road
Highlights: Panoramic views of the Grapevine Mountains
Flowers: April–June
Best light: Early morning
Elevation: 5,100'

White Pass provides the first of many panoramic views of the Grapevine Mountains, with its multicolored rock strata overlooking a wide valley—actually the upper part of Titanothere Canyon. Fossil beds in this area are 30 to 35 million years old; in 1933 the skull of a titanothere, a large prehistoric mammal related to horses and rhinos, was found here.

Hike up the trail to the right of the road about 100 yards and you'll find a place where the ground has been worn smooth by photographers' feet—and for good reason: the view here is wonderful. Look ahead and see how the road snakes its way through the flat part of the valley, then seems to disappear into the steep canyon.

Just after the pass, the road becomes steeper and narrower and can be dangerously slick in wet weather. If it's raining at this point, turn around.

17 Red Pass

Mile 12.4, Titus Canyon Road
Highlights: Panoramic views of the Grapevine Mountains
Flowers: April–June
Best light: Early morning
Elevation: 5,250'

Shooting from the top of Thimble Peak, you might have a chance to make eye contact with a soaring turkey vulture. Left: DSLR, 35-70mm lens at 35mm, 1/200 sec, f13, ISO 200. Right: DSLR, 300mm lens, 1/1000 sec, f5, ISO 200.

Red sandstone and steep cliffs make this a popular spot for photographers as well as geologists. There are two places to park here, each big enough for two cars, and on some weekends in winter or early spring all four spaces might be taken.

Hike up to the right (north) of the road to photograph the square, banded rock formations. Keep climbing for a panoramic view that includes the road and canyon ahead of you as well as the canyon you just drove through.

This is the highest point on Titus Canyon Road; from here you start the long descent into Titus Canyon.

18 Thimble Peak

4-mile hike (round trip) starts at Red Pass, mile 12.4, Titus Canyon Road
Highlights: Views of Death Valley and the Grapevine Mountains, hiking
Flowers: April–June

Best light: Early morning, late afternoon
Elevation: 5,250 to 6,381'

I only recently discovered this trail, and after hiking it just once I can say it's one of my favorite desert hikes. It combines the sweeping vistas of mountain hiking with the wide-open spaces of the desert as you hike along a ridge to one of the highest peaks in the Grapevine Mountains.

The trail doesn't appear to be heavily used; when I hiked it I saw more bighorn sheep prints than human footprints. It's a good idea to carry a compass or GPS on this hike, especially for the return trip. You don't want to hike back on the wrong ridge and lose your way.

From Red Pass, climb the roadcut to the left of the road—the easiest place is just opposite the second parking space, on the far side of the hairpin turn. Continue hiking south along the ridge as you climb several rounded hills. As you reach the top of the

It's not exactly easy, but I think you'll agree the 360-degree view makes this hike worth the effort.

19 Leadfield

Mile 15.5, Titus Canyon Road
Highlights: Ghost town, reptiles
Flowers: April–May
Best light: Late afternoon
Elevation: 4,000'

Walking around Leadfield, you get a very real sense of the isolation experienced by the 300 or so people who moved here in 1926 with great hopes for their future—and abandoned the town barely six months later. Shooting the remaining buildings with a wide-angle lens, including the surrounding desert, conveys that feeling of isolation and loneliness. In addition to wide-angle views, the details in rusted metal and weathered wood provide opportunities to experiment with shadows and textures.

Zebra-tailed lizards are common around the ruins, and chuckwallas live on the surrounding rocks. You can easily spend a couple hours here.

There are open mines in this area, and I strongly recommend that you stay out of them. They haven't been maintained since the miners left, and you never know when a rotten timber will give way or a rock wall will collapse. Or, for that matter, when you'll fall into an unseen vertical shaft or run into a rattlesnake that's using the mine as a daytime resting place.

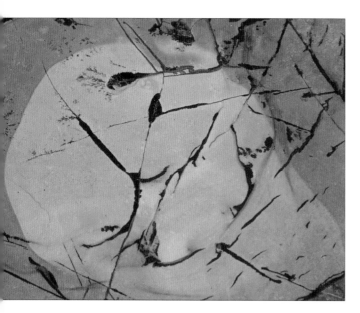

Close-ups of rocks can reveal beautiful colors and patterns. 35mm Ektachrome 100VS film, 105mm lens, ISO 100, exposure data not recorded.

second hill, Thimble Peak will come into view on your right. The trail is generally well-defined but it does fade out occasionally where the ground is especially rocky. If you lose the trail, don't worry; just keep heading south along the ridge and you'll find it again.

After about a mile you'll reach an overlook with some large rock outcrops and a view of Death Valley. Take a break here and enjoy the view—but there's an even better view to come. To your right is a large saddle with Thimble Peak on the other side. Cross the saddle and climb the north face of the peak. The last stretch, maybe a couple hundred feet, is a scramble—you'll need both hands—with occasional loose rocks that can be especially dangerous on the way down.

⑳ Klare Spring

Mile 18, Titus Canyon Road
Highlights: Petroglyphs, flowers,
**   occasional bighorn sheep**
Flowers: March–May
Best light: Late afternoon
Elevation: 3,200'

A sign on your right describes the petroglyphs in this area. When you photograph the petroglyphs, don't touch them and don't climb on the rocks—these remnants of an ancient civilization are thousands of years old and can't be replaced. Shooting petroglyphs can be a challenge, because they blend with the rocks and are often hard to "read" in a photo. I usually find I need to increase contrast when processing the image.

Just past the petroglyphs is Klare Spring, a wet spot at the side of the road that is in fact the biggest source of water in the Titus Canyon area. Desert bighorn sheep rely on the spring, especially in the summer months, and it's not unusual to find their footprints or droppings nearby. If you're lucky you might get to see a small band of sheep, but don't count on it. They only need to visit the spring every few days and are wary about approaching it if anyone is around. If you do see sheep, stay back and use a telephoto lens.

Look carefully in the vegetation along the spring and you might find stream orchids, the only orchid native to the California deserts. Harsh light can make the orchids diffi-

Prince's plume framed by the narrow walls of Titus Canyon. Keeping the background out of focus ensures that the fine lines of the flower will stand out. DSLR, 105mm lens, 1/200 sec, f9, ISO 100.

cult to photograph, so you will need to use a reflector or fill-flash to soften the shadows.

Below Klare Spring the canyon starts to get narrower and steeper, with heavy shade on one side or the other.

Yelloweye lupine in Wildrose Canyon. DSLR, 105mm lens, 1/500 sec, f8, ISO 200.

21 Titus Canyon Narrows

Mile 22, Titus Canyon Road
Highlights: Steep, narrow canyon,
    interesting geology
Flowers: February–April
Best light: It's complicated
Elevation: 1,000'

Here the canyon narrows dramatically, its near-vertical sides at times less than 20 feet apart and hundreds of feet high. Spend a few minutes here and you'll feel like a tourist in Manhattan, staring up at the rock walls with your mouth slightly open. (You might also join the thousands before you who have suddenly noticed that "Titus Canyon" sounds a lot like "tight-ass canyon.")

In the canyon walls you'll see intricate breccia mosaics and contrasting rock strata, all created by millions of years of geologic forces including pressure, temperature, folding, faulting, and erosion. Your photographic challenge here will be the extreme contrast of light and shadow; at least one wall of the canyon will be shaded most of the time. Experiment with different exposures, or if you like a technical approach you can try some HDR processing.

Just as abruptly as it began, the narrow canyon ends when it opens onto an alluvial fan on the east side of Death Valley. Continue on the dirt road to rejoin the main highway about halfway between Grapevine Ranger Station and Stovepipe Wells Village.

21 Titus Canyon Narrows — the easy way

Highlights: Steep, narrow canyon,
    interesting geology
Flowers: February–April
Best light: It's complicated
Elevation: 1,000'
Access: 2.5-mile dirt road,
    short walk into the canyon

A borax wagon at Harmony Borax Works. Shooting through the fence with a wide-angle lens makes the wagon look less like a museum exhibit and adds an interesting perspective. DSLR, 10-24mm lens at 10mm, 1/200 sec, f14, ISO 200.

If you don't have time for the entire Titus Canyon Road, you can drive to the bottom of Titus Canyon via the exit road off the main park road. From the parking area you can walk a short distance up the canyon to the narrows.

Directions: Turn off on the E side of the main park road about 15 miles N of SR190, or 18 miles S of Grapevine Ranger Station.

● Emigrant

190

to Stovepipe Wells

Mustard Canyon 23
Harmony Borax Works 22
Furnace Creek 24

50 Skidoo

Golden Canyon 30   25 Zabriskie Point
Mushroom Rock 31   26 Twenty Mule Team Canyon

Eureka Mine
51   52 Aguereberry Point
53 Emigrant Pass   Salt Flats 47

32 Artist's Palette

48 Devil's Golf Course

56 Wildrose Peak
54 Wildrose Campground   Devil's Golf Course 33   34 Natural Bridge
55 Charcoal Kilns
Mahogany Flat 57   Hanaupah Canyon
43

35 Badwater

27 Dante's View

49 Eagle Borax Works

58 Telescope Peak

West Side Road 46

28 Greenwater Valley

36 Mormon Point

44 Warm Spring Canyon

45 Butte Valley

Ashford Mill 37   38 Jubilee Pass

373

Ash Meadows
29

127

to Las Vegas →

190

Death Valley Junction

178

Shoshon

Salsberry Pass 39

127

North ↑
0 1   5   10 Kilometers
0 1   5   10 Miles

Ibex Dunes
41

Saratoga Spring
40

Salt Creek Hills 42

to Baker →

South

This is the busiest and most developed area of the park. Restaurants, lodging, restrooms, camping, a gas station, and even a golf course (a real one, not the Devil's Golf Course) are all available at Furnace Creek. Just outside the park, a full range of services can be found in Shoshone. Restrooms or pit toilets are located at some of the more popular features, including Dante's View (at the trailer parking area), Badwater, Zabriskie Point, and Ash Meadows.

22 Harmony Borax Works

Highlights: History, borax wagon, other equipment
Flowers: February–March
Best light: Early morning, late afternoon
Elevation: -200'
Access: Short dirt road, easy self-guided walk

Known as the birthplace of the iconic Twenty Mule Teams, the refinery here operated for only five years, from 1883 to 1888. At its peak, the plant produced three tons of borax per day and employed 40 men, about three quarters of them Chinese immigrants. The huge wagons each held ten tons of borax and were hauled in pairs, along with a 500-gallon water wagon, by teams that actually consisted of 18 mules and two horses. Fully loaded, the rig weighed 30 tons and was pulled 165 miles to Mojave, where the animals and crew had just one night to rest before returning for another load. (In fact, it was probably just the animals who rested; the crew was more likely to spend most of the night, and all of their pay, in the saloons and brothels.)

Interpretive signs along the self-guided walking tour give a very brief overview of the operation and the workers' lives. Photo subjects here include an original borax wagon, the ruins of a few buildings, and the big steam boiler—17 feet long and 4 feet in diameter—that heated the refining tanks and powered the machinery.

The borax wagon is behind a rail fence, so it's difficult to get a shot of the whole thing without making it look like a museum exhibit. On the other hand, there are none of the "keep off" signs that adorn the wagons at Furnace Creek. I like to focus on the details: the spokes and hubs of the wheels, the texture of the wood, or the rusted hardware.

Directions: 2 miles N of Furnace Creek on SR190.

23 Mustard Canyon

Highlights: Colorful canyon, erosion patterns
Flowers: February–March
Best light: Early morning, late afternoon
Elevation: -200'
Access: 2-mile one-way dirt road

Continuing past Harmony Borax Works, the road winds past the yellow cliffs of Mustard Canyon. Colored by borates and oxidized iron, this small range of low hills has been eroded into shapes and patterns that vary

Manly Beacon at Zabriskie Point, one of the iconic views of Death Valley. For the best light, shoot at sunrise. DSLR, 70-300mm lens at 100mm, 1/80 sec, f16, ISO 100.

with each turn of the road. You can stop almost anywhere and find an interesting photo subject, whether you're shooting detailed close-ups or larger landscapes.

As with any canyon, one side or the other will likely be in shadow in early morning or late afternoon when the light is best. What's different here, though, is that the color of the rock can take on a warm glow even in mid-afternoon, so you can shoot some appealing landscapes at a time of day when both sides of the canyon are in full light. (The same is true at Zabriskie Point and in Twenty Mule Team Canyon.)

Directions: 2 miles N of Furnace Creek on SR190, turn off the highway onto the dirt road and continue past Harmony Borax Works.

24 Furnace Creek

Highlights: Visitor Center, history, birds; also food, gas, lodging, and shopping
Flowers: February–March
Best light: Late afternoon
Elevation: -200'
Access: Paved road

This is the hub of human activity in the park, a place to stop for gas, ice, food, and whatever else you might need. If it's your first visit I highly recommend spending some time at the Visitor Center; the exhibits will give you a good sense of Death Valley's history, and you can browse an extensive selection of books and maps. The store at Furnace Creek Ranch carries a variety of T-shirts and other souvenirs, as well as books, DVDs, and even some food items. You'll also have a choice of restaurants and lodging, including the historic (and expensive) Furnace Creek Inn.

There are two original borax wagons here; neither is fenced, but both have "keep off" signs on them, which can limit your photo compositions. I prefer to shoot the wagon at Harmony Borax Works (p. 75)—even though there's a fence around it, there are no signs to distract from the wagon itself.

Hikers in Twenty Mule Team Canyon stop to admire their shadows. DSLR, 18-70mm lens at 52mm, 1/160 sec, f11, ISO 100.

The palms, tamarisks, mesquites, and other trees at Furnace Creek, along with natural and man-made water sources, attract a variety of birds to the area. On Airport Road, which starts near the Visitor Center, there's a birdwatching platform overlooking a pond at the edge of the golf course. If you have a spotting scope or a good pair of binoculars this can be a good place to observe waterfowl, but it's not really close enough for photography.

Directions: SR190 near the center of the park.

25 Zabriskie Point

Highlights: Colorful eroded badlands, hiking
Flowers: Not likely
Best light: Early morning, late afternoon
Elevation: 700'
Access: Paved road, short walk up the hill to the observation area

Photos from Zabriskie Point, an iconic image of Death Valley, have been published in countless books, magazines, posters, and calendars. The view here is one of the best

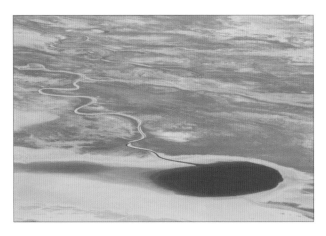

Left: When you're shooting from Dante's View, use a telephoto lens to isolate patterns in the valley floor. DSLR, 70-300mm lens at 200mm, 1/250 sec, f18, ISO 200.   **Right:** Seen from Dante's View, the first light of sunrise strikes Telescope Peak and the Panamint Range. DSLR, 80-400mm lens at 116mm, 1/40 sec, f8, ISO 100.

examples of eroded badlands you'll find anywhere, a profusion of color and texture that can keep a photographer busy all day. Manly Beacon, the distinctive peak to the west of the viewing area, is one of the most recognizable features in the park. The best colors, and the highest concentration of photographers, will be on display around sunrise and sunset. In spite of the occasional crowds, I've found photographers here to be considerate about not stepping into each other's photos.

The view can be so striking here, it's hard to know where to begin. At the same time, you're often surrounded by other photographers, so you might be feeling some pressure to make a photo that doesn't look just like everyone else's. I like to use a longer lens and isolate the details, maybe highlighting the way a single ridge is divided into light and shadow, or looking for unexpected patterns of color or texture. For a re-

ally special view, plan to be here at sunrise just as the full moon is setting over the Panamints. To get a close-up look at the badlands, you can hike the trail from Zabriskie Point to Golden Canyon (p. 82).

Directions: 4 miles SE of Furnace Creek on SR190.

26 Twenty Mule Team Canyon

Highlights: Colorful eroded badlands, hiking
Flowers: Not likely
Best light: Early morning, late afternoon
Elevation: 1,000'
Access: 3-mile dirt road; hiking optional

Like nearby Zabriskie Point and Golden Canyon, the badlands here are especially beautiful just before sunset. And unlike those locations, you can often explore here without the company of other photographers. Here, away from the crowds of Zabriskie Point, I often feel more free to move around and explore shooting from different perspectives and directions, without worrying that I'm wandering into someone else's photo or that someone else will walk into my photo.

The one-way road winds through yellow hills of eroded lakebed deposits. You can stop almost anywhere along the road and hike up along the ridges, where creative compositions can be found in any direction. Hiking along certain ridges in late afternoon, you might feel like you have a companion—your shadow will appear to be hiking on the next ridge to the east.

Directions: 5 miles SE of Furnace Creek on SR190.

27 Dante's View

Highlights: Panoramic views of Death Valley
Flowers: April–June
Best light: Early morning
Elevation: 5,475'
Access: Steep, winding paved road; trailers and vehicles over 25 feet prohibited for the last 6 miles

Big Spring in Ash Meadows National Wildlife Refuge. DSLR, 18-70mm lens at 27mm, 1/200 sec, f7.1, ISO 100.

In the warm light of sunset, it's easy to see how Golden Canyon and Red Cathedral got their names. DSLR, 10-24mm lens at 17mm, 1/200 sec, f13, ISO 200.

From more than a mile above the valley floor, Dante's View provides a striking panorama of Death Valley. You can shoot from the overlook at the parking area or walk the trails to the north or south; you'll find great views whichever you choose.

Look to the west and you see Telescope Peak and the Panamint Range rising dramatically above Badwater Basin. On a very clear day you can see Mt. Whitney, in the southern Sierra about 100 miles away—giving you a view of both the highest and lowest points in the contiguous 48 states. To the north and south, Death Valley seems to stretch out forever in both directions. Don't forget to look to the east as well, for a view of the Greenwater Range.

Early morning is the best time to photograph the Panamint Range and its massive alluvial fans, as well as the sunrise over the Greenwater Range. Remember to bring a warm coat and a sturdy tripod—it can get pretty cold at that elevation, and it's almost always windy.

While you're shooting panoramic views, don't forget the details as well—the intricate patterns and winding channels made by seasonal water on the salt pan, the alluvial fans that spill out onto the valley floor—whatever speaks to your personal vision.

Directions: From Furnace Creek, 11 miles SE on SR190; turn right on Dante's View Road for 13 miles. About 6 miles below Dante's View is a parking area where you can unhitch your trailer and continue to the top without it.

28 Greenwater Valley

Highlights: Flowers, wildlife
Flowers: March–May
Best light: Early morning, late afternoon
Elevation: 2,200 to 4,000'
Access: 30-mile dirt road, may be rough—ask about current conditions

Greenwater Valley is a good example of mid-elevation creosote bush desert, and one of the less-used areas of the park. The road is usually in pretty good condition, and in the spring it can be a great place to spend a leisurely morning or afternoon photographing wildflowers, driving slowly and stopping whenever you see something you like. Horned lizards, gopher snakes, jackrabbits, coyotes, and other wildlife may be seen here as well.

Directions: From Furnace Creek, 11 miles SE on SR190; turn right on Dante's View Road for 7.5 miles to the trailer parking area where the dirt road starts. From Shoshone, 1.7 miles N on SR127; then W on SR178 for 5.8 miles; turn right on Furnace Creek Wash Road.

29 Ash Meadows National Wildlife Refuge

Highlights: Birds, reptiles, springs, pupfish
Flowers: March–April
Best light: Early morning, late afternoon (varies with specific location)
Elevation: 2,300'
Access: Gravel roads

Mushroom Rock seems to change shape as you view it from different angles. Use the northern sky as a background for the most dramatic photos. DSLR, 18-70mm lens at 27mm, 1/125 sec, f7.1, ISO 100.

Driving toward Death Valley from the Las Vegas area, you might pass a turnoff for Ash Meadows National Wildlife Refuge. Or you might be curious about a dot on the map labeled "Devil's Hole Death Valley National Park." That curiosity can lead you to discover this 23,000-acre preserve established in 1984 in the southern Amargosa Desert. The refuge is said to have the greatest concentration of endemic species of any similar-sized area in the United States.

Highlights include a boardwalk trail at Crystal Springs, with interpretive signs that provide an introduction to the refuge, and Point of Rocks Spring, where Ash Meadows pupfish are most easily seen and photographed. (See p. 43 for tips on photographing pupfish.) The hills above Point of Rocks Spring are good for off-trail hiking and provide an overview of the refuge.

Devil's Hole, the only habitat of Devil's Hole pupfish, is a 400-foot-deep cavern with a small opening at the base of a hill. The fish live and breed on a small rock shelf, about 6 by 12 feet, near the surface of the 90-degree water. The opening is fenced off, and only accessible to researchers, so you won't be able to see these fish. While it's inside the National Wildlife Refuge, Devil's Hole is managed by Death Valley National Park.

Directions: From Death Valley Junction, E on State Line Road (called Ash Meadows Road on some maps) 6.2 miles to the refuge entrance.

㉚ Golden Canyon

Highlights: Colorful canyon views, hiking
Flowers: February–March
Best light: Late afternoon
Elevation: Sea level to 600'
Access: Paved road; moderate 4- to 10-mile hike (round trip)

This is the back door to Zabriskie Point (p. 77)—a hike through the golden badlands surrounding Manly Beacon. While Zabriskie Point gives you the bigger picture, this hike is where you'll get up close and personal with the colors and textures of the badlands. Late afternoon sunlight brings out the color and bathes the entire canyon in a warm glow.

A trail guide is available in the parking area, although many of the numbered markers along the trail were missing the last time I hiked the canyon. At about the one-mile point, the trail branches, with the right fork leading to Zabriskie Point (1.5 miles) and the left to Red Cathedral (¼ mile), a beautiful natural amphitheater. There are many unmarked branches of the canyon as well, so it's best to allow plenty of time for exploration.

In the upper parts of the canyon are dry falls, twisting, narrow passageways, and eroded rocks of all shapes and textures. The contrast between the red cliffs of Red Cathedral and the yellow badlands around Manly Beacon is especially intriguing. Beautiful photos are waiting to be made in every direction.

Directions: 3 miles S of Furnace Creek on Badwater Road.

The arches and other shapes at Devil's Golf Course sometimes resemble Utah's canyonlands, but on a much smaller scale. The hole in this arch is about the size of my fist. DSLR, 10-24mm lens at 10mm, 1/200 sec, f13, ISO 200.

㉛ Mushroom Rock

Highlights: Oddly shaped rock, flowers
Flowers: February–March
Best light: Late afternoon
Elevation: -200'
Access: Paved road

One of the most photographed rocks in the park, this fine example of eroded basalt seems to change its shape as you view it from different directions. Lie on the ground and shoot it against the northern sky for the most dramatic composition. Whatever you do, don't climb on the rock. Others have tried that, and parts of it have broken off under their weight, which is why there's no longer a sign to tell you where it is.

The area around Mushroom Rock, especially to the north, can be a very good early spring wildflower location.

Directions: 5.5 miles S of Furnace Creek on Badwater Road.

Left: Over six inches of rain fell in the 2004-05 season, turning Badwater into a temporary lake. DSLR, 70-300mm lens at 135mm, 1/500 sec, f18, ISO 200.

Look up from Badwater and you'll see the sign on the cliff indicating sea level, 282 feet above you. **Right**: DSLR, 18-70mm lens at 40mm, 1/200 sec, f9, ISO 100. **Above**: DSLR, 70-300mm lens at 300mm, 1/200 sec, f8, ISO 100.

㉜ Artist's Drive and Artist's Palette

Highlights: Colorful geology, hiking
Flowers: February–March
Best light: Late afternoon
Elevation: -200 to 800'
Access: Paved road; hiking optional; trailers and vehicles over 25 feet not allowed

This nine-mile one-way loop takes you through an especially colorful area of volcanic and sedimentary rock at the base of the Amargosa Range. The cliffs face west, making late afternoon the best time for photography. The main attraction—that is, the place where everyone stops for photos—is Artist's Palette, where there's a small parking lot facing the most colorful area. But don't neglect the rest of the drive—there are many other places to find photos.

On the first half of the drive, just past the first of two big dips in the road, you'll find lots of interesting geology on the west side of the road as well as great color in the cliffs east of the road. There are plenty of good places to shoot on the second half of the drive as well, after you pass Artist's Palette and the road winds through the hills on your way back to Badwater Road. It would be impossible to list every good photo location on this drive—and there's no need to, because you'll recognize them when you see them.

Directions: Loop road starts 10 miles S of Furnace Creek on Badwater Road.

㉝ Devil's Golf Course (Badwater Road)

Highlights: Wind- and rain-sculpted salt formations
Flowers: Not likely
Best light: Early morning, late afternoon
Elevation: -200'
Access: 1.5-mile dirt road; short walk over rough ground

I'm not a golfer, but I can understand the reasoning behind the name of this feature. A person can barely walk here; playing golf would be impossible. It's a large flat area of rock salt that's been eroded by rain and wind into bizarre jagged shapes.

On a typical day, car after car will drive in, the driver and passengers will get out for a few photos, and then it's back in the car and on to the next stop. Nobody seems to walk more than about ten feet from the parking area, and everyone gets the same shot. You, of course, want something a little more interesting or creative.

Walk out past the footprints, and you'll find that the salt formations are dramatically different where they haven't been crushed under everyone's shoes. Here's where you can make some interesting photos. Shooting from eye level may not convey the jaggedness of the surface; for a better perspective, get down low and focus on the details. In close-up, some of the shapes look like miniature versions of the arches and hoodoos of Utah's Canyonlands.

Directions: 12 miles S of Furnace Creek on Badwater Road. See also location 48 on West Side Road, p. 95.

34 Natural Bridge

Highlights: Canyon views, hiking
Flowers: February–March
Best light: Late afternoon
Elevation: 1,000'
Access: 1.5-mile gravel road; 1- to 2-mile
hike (round trip)

This arch—one of only a few in the Death Valley area—spans a narrow canyon on the western slope of the Black Mountains. While it lacks the drama or gracefulness of Utah's better-known arches, you can still make some good photos here. For the best views, keep hiking past the arch and shoot it from a little farther up the canyon.

Continue hiking to photograph the dry falls, polished smooth by occasional rain and flash floods. At about the one-mile point the trail ends, blocked by a much higher and steeper dry fall.

Back at the parking area, the alluvial fan below the arch provides some great early morning views of the salt pan around Badwater. The fan here is also a good early spring wildflower location.

Directions: 15 miles S of Furnace Creek on Badwater Road.

35 Badwater

Highlights: Lowest elevation in U.S.;
water, salt flats
Flowers: Not likely
Best light: Late afternoon
Elevation: -282'
Access: Paved road; short walk to water
and salt flats

Everyone stops at Badwater because it's the lowest point in the United States, but most people don't walk very far toward the salt flats—and that's where the real photos are. Standing in this vast white plain (the salt pan covers 200 square miles) you get a ground-level appreciation of Death Valley's size. Use a wide-angle lens for a perspective that seems to go on forever. In wet years the salt flats can become a lake and a rare opportunity to shoot the Panamint Mountains reflected in water.

From the salt flats, look back toward the parking area and find the "sea level" sign. You may be surprised how far up the cliff it is. Farther up the mountain is Dante's View, more than a mile above you.

Directions: 17 miles S of Furnace Creek on Badwater Road.

Desert gold at the south end of Death Valley near Ashford Mill. DSLR, 17-35mm lens at 24mm, 1/250 sec, f13, ISO 200.

36 Mormon Point and other Badwater Road locations

Highlights: Flowers, views of Death Valley and the surrounding mountains
Flowers: February–March
Best light: Late afternoon
Elevation: -200'
Access: Paved road

Driving north on Badwater Road as it winds along the base of the Amargosa Range, you'll see some great views of the mountains and canyons ahead of you. One of the best places to stop for a photo is Mormon Point, which is also a good wildflower location in most years.

Mormon Point is just one of my favorite spots; you'll find many others all along the road between Ashford Mill and Furnace Creek. All of these locations along the east side of the valley will receive their best light in late afternoon.

Directions: 15 miles S of Badwater on Badwater Road.

Jubilee Pass and Emigrant Pass are both excellent wildflower locations and have beautiful light at sunset.

Above: Jubilee Pass.
DSLR, 70-300mm lens at 70mm, 1/500 sec, f10, ISO 200.

Below: Emigrant Pass.
DSLR, 10-24mm lens at 15mm, 1/200 sec, f6.3, ISO 200.

 Ashford Mill

Highlights: Ruins of old mill
Flowers: February–March
Best light: Early morning, late afternoon
Elevation: -100'
Access: ¼-mile dirt road

Harold Ashford and his brothers never gave up on their dream of getting rich here, but as with most of Death Valley's prospectors, their plans didn't quite work out that way. Despite having processed nearly $125,000 worth of gold from nearby mines, the mill never did make a profit. One author has called it "Death Valley's most conspicuous monument to disappointment."

Like most mill sites, Ashford sits on a low hill, which allowed for easier loading of ore at the upper end and unloading at the lower end. The hill faces south and overlooks a broad wash, so the site has good light in both morning and afternoon. The ruins consist of a single small concrete building, of which only three walls remain, and the wood and concrete foundation of the mill itself.

Directions: 45 miles S of Furnace Creek on Badwater Road.

③⑧ Jubilee Pass ③⑨ Salsberry Pass

Highlights: Panoramic views, flowers
Flowers: March–May
Best light: Late afternoon at Jubilee; early morning and late afternoon at Salsberry
Elevation: Jubilee 1,290', Salsberry 3,315'
Access: Paved road

Top: Just after sunset, the evening sky is reflected in Saratoga Spring. 35mm Ektachrome 64X film, 55mm lens, ISO 64, exposure data not recorded.

Bottom: Saratoga Spring is an important area for migrating waterfowl, including this Canada goose. 35mm Ektachrome 64X film, ISO 64, lens and exposure data not recorded.

If you take the southern route in or out of Death Valley, these passes will be part of your first or last view of the park—and if you time it right, they can be beautiful bookends to your trip. On my most recent visit I spent a night in Shoshone so I could get an early start and catch the first light of dawn on Salsberry Pass.

Both passes, as well as the valley between them, receive a little more rainfall than nearby areas, making them good wildflower locations. Thanks to their elevation and orientation, they both receive good light in late afternoon; of the two, Salsberry receives better morning light.

From Salsberry Pass, walk a couple hundred yards north of the road for some great views to the east or west. South of the road the views are to the west; here you'll find more interesting geology, with some very intriguing rock formations.

Jubilee Pass is beautiful in late afternoon, especially in spring, when the flowers and hillsides seem to glow with the golden light of sunset. Walk up the hills on either side of the road for some fantastic views.

Directions: SR178; Salsberry Pass is 10 miles W of Shoshone; Jubilee Pass is 21 miles W of Shoshone.

㊵ Saratoga Spring

Highlights: Birds, water, reptiles, hiking
Flowers: February–April
Best light: Late afternoon
Elevation: 200'
Access: 10-mile dirt road, may be rough; short walk to the spring

Sunset warms the colors of the Ibex Dunes and Saddle Peak Hills. 35mm Ektachrome 64X film, 200mm lens, 1/30 sec, f8, ISO 64.

More than 150 species of birds have been recorded at this 15-acre oasis, including many spring and fall migrants stopping for a much needed rest on their long journeys north or south. The ponds here are also home to the Saratoga Spring pupfish, an endemic reminder of a time when the entire valley was covered by a vast lake. Sit quietly at the edge of the pond, and you can watch the brightly colored males defending their territories and trying to attract females. (See p. 43 for advice on shooting pupfish.)

For a beautiful sunset with the wetland in the foreground, climb up the steep, rocky slope of the Ibex Hills overlooking the spring. Or for an alternative view, walk around to the far side of the spring and shoot toward the hills, as the setting sun warms the colors of both the hills and the marsh plants.

Spring snowmelt in the Panamint Range leads to wildflowers in Hanaupah Canyon, including this brittlebush. 35mm Ektachrome 64X film, ISO 64, lens and exposure data not recorded.

Directions: From Shoshone, S on SR127 for 24 miles; turn right at the historical marker on Harry Wade Road. (From Baker, the turnoff is about 32 miles N, on your left.) Continue W for about 6 miles; turn right for another 2.7 miles; turn left and go another 1.2 miles.

41 Ibex Dunes

Highlights: Sand dunes, reptiles, hiking
Flowers: February–April
Best light: Early morning, late afternoon
Elevation: 400'
Access: 10-mile dirt road, may be rough; 4-mile hike (round trip) plus hiking on the dunes
Alternate access: Paved road; 8-mile hike (round trip) plus hiking on the dunes

All of the sand dunes in the park are beautiful, but to me the Ibex Dunes always stand out as special. Somehow the alignment and shape of these dunes, the color of the sand, and the direction of the light have all combined in just the right way to make a photographer happy.

There are no trails here. To reach the dunes you need to walk across open desert for two to four miles (depending on where you start), so make sure you carry plenty of water. A good flashlight and a compass or GPS are essential, too—if you want to shoot these dunes at sunset, you'll be walking back to your car in the dark.

As you approach the dunes you pass through creosote bush scrub, which becomes more sparse as the soil gets sandier around the base of the dunes. Desert iguanas are abundant in this area, and in early spring the delicate lavender flowers of sand verbena add unexpected color to the transition zone. A few hardy creosotes grow on the dunes themselves, providing shelter for sidewinders and fringe-toed lizards.

Directions: From Shoshone, S on SR127 for 24 miles; turn right at the historical marker on Harry Wade Road. (From Baker, the turnoff is about 32 miles N, on your left.) Continue W for about 6 miles, then turn right for another 4 miles or so, keeping to the right at the turnoff for Saratoga Spring. The dunes will be visible on your right; when the road starts to curve slightly left, away from the dunes, park your car and start hiking about 2 miles to the dunes. Caution: If you continue driving on this road you could become stuck in deep sand.

Alternate directions: Park on SR127 just N of the Dumont Dunes turnoff and hike about 4 miles W, around the base of the Saddle Peak Hills.

42 Salt Creek Hills

Highlights: Birds, water, hiking
Flowers: February–March
Best light: Late afternoon
Elevation: 600'
Access: Paved road; short hike to the spring

Often overlooked (it's outside the park), the BLM-managed Salt Creek Hills Area of Critical Environmental Concern—called Salt Spring Hills on some maps—is worth stopping for, especially in winter or early

Old mining equipment in Warm Spring Canyon. 35mm Ektachrome 100VS film, ISO 100, lens and exposure data not recorded.

spring. Like nearby Saratoga Spring, it includes several acres of marshland and is an important habitat for over 150 species of birds. Most of the non-native tamarisk trees that once choked off the flow of water have been removed in an effort to restore the marsh to its original condition. The tamarisks that remain provide shade as well as photo opportunities.

The trail from the parking area leads around a rocky hill to a series of overlooks where you can photograph the marsh or watch for birds in the grasses that grow to over six feet tall. Continue along the trail across the wash to the remaining grove of tamarisks.

Directions: From Shoshone, 25 miles S on SR127; turnoff is on the E side of the road.

Above: Sunrise in Butte Valley, reflected in the window of the Geologist's Cabin. 35mm Ektachrome 100VS film, 20mm lens, ISO 100, exposure data not recorded.   **Below:** At sunset, the shadows on Striped Butte in Butte Valley create the image of a face. 35mm Ektachrome 100VS film, 70-300mm lens, ISO 100, focal length and exposure data not recorded.

43 Hanaupah Canyon

Highlights: Canyon views, water, birds, reptiles, hiking

Flowers: March–May

Best light: Early morning

Elevation: 5,000'

Access: 11-mile gravel road plus very rough 8-mile 4WD road; closed in summer; entire route may not be passable even in the best conditions

Hanaupah is one of my favorite canyons; it's a rough, slow drive, but worth it, especially in springtime. The upper part of the canyon carries snowmelt from Telescope Peak, ensuring a good wildflower bloom in most years. After the "road" ends (or when you start to worry about getting stuck), continue hiking up the canyon to find waterfalls cascading over the rocks and even a small population of treefrogs—not what you'd expect in Death Valley. The best light in Hanaupah occurs in the early morning.

Directions: From Furnace Creek, 7 miles S on Badwater Road; turn right on West Side Road for about 11 miles; turn right at the sign for Hanaupah Canyon. Requires high-clearance 4WD; be sure to ask about current conditions first.

44 Warm Spring Canyon

Highlights: Canyon views, water, birds, reptiles, ruins of old mining equipment
Flowers: March–May
Best light: Early morning
Elevation: 2,600'
Access: Up to 33 miles of gravel road plus 13-mile dirt road; closed in summer

Here you'll find an old mining camp, some abandoned equipment that was once used to process ore, and even a spring-fed swimming pool. (Last time I was there the pool had been drained. I guess it was considered a safety hazard, but it was fun while it lasted.) Above the mining camp, follow the spring to its source, where you'll find wild grapevines clinging to the steep cliff.

During the spring bloom, shooting delicate, colorful wildflowers in contrast with the stark, rusty mining equipment can make a dramatic photo. Because this canyon faces east, the best light will be in the early morning.

Directions: From Furnace Creek, 7 miles S on Badwater Road; turn right on West Side Road for about 33 miles; turn right at the sign for Warm Spring Canyon.

Alternate directions (more paved road, less gravel): From Furnace Creek, 44 miles S on Badwater Road to the S end of West Side Road; turn right and go N on West Side Road for 3 miles; turn left at the sign for Warm Spring Canyon.

45 Butte Valley

Highlights: Old cabins, reptiles, panoramic views, hiking
Flowers: April–May
Best light: Early morning, late afternoon
Elevation: 3,700'
Access: 23-mile rough dirt road; requires high-clearance 4WD for the last 10 miles

If you're really feeling adventurous, continue up Warm Spring Canyon to Butte Valley, a beautiful place to explore in the middle of the Panamint Range. Watch for desert mariposa lilies on the north side of the road, just before you get to Butte Valley. In and around the valley you'll find a variety of wildflowers and lizards.

At least three old cabins are tucked away here, each with its own fascinating history. The Geologist's Cabin, a one-room stone building on the hill above Anvil Spring, has become an informal guest house. If you stay there, be sure to clean up after your-self, pack out your trash, write a note in the guest book, and leave something for the next visitor: canned food, a favorite book, anything to contribute to the sense of community. Make sure you get up early enough to shoot the sunrise—you won't want to miss it here.

Striped Butte (you'll know it when you see it) sits at the northern end of the valley; you can hike to the top for a good view. The hill above the Geologist's Cabin has an even better view. In the evening, watch how the changing light and shadow on Striped Butte creates the image of a face.

Directions: Continue up Warm Spring Canyon (p. 93) for 10 miles past the old min-ing camp. Requires high-clearance 4WD; be sure to ask about current conditions first.

46 West Side Road

Highlights: Salt flats, birds, marsh, insects, history
Flowers: February–April
Best light: Early morning, late afternoon
Elevation: -200'
Access: Gravel road

This 36-mile gravel road branches off of Badwater Road and runs along the west-ern edge of southern Death Valley, provid-ing access to several historic and natural sites as well as the canyons of the Pana-mint Range. The entire road is about 200 feet below sea level.

There are no facilities along the road. The nearest restaurants, lodging, camping, and

The marsh at Eagle Borax Works is excellent habitat for birds and insects. DSLR, 10-24mm lens at 15mm, 1/200 sec, f13, ISO 200.

gas stations are at Furnace Creek and Sho-shone.

Directions: North end of the road starts at Badwater Road about 7 miles S of Furnace Creek, near Artist's Drive. South end is at Badwater Road 25 miles S of Badwater. Mile-age for locations 47–49 is measured from the north end of West Side Road.

47 Salt Flats

Mile 1.8, West Side Road

If you've never seen it before, Death Valley's salt pan might surprise you—it's not com-pletely flat, but instead has a mosaic pat-tern, as though made of giant white tiles with ridges between them. The salt dissolves in wet weather and then expands as it dries, forcing the ridges higher as more water evap-orates.

This is my favorite location to photograph the salt pan, especially at sunrise. The first light of morning warms the colors of the Panamint Mountains, while the sun's low angle emphasizes the roughly hexagonal shapes. Park in one of the turnouts and walk about 10 or 15 minutes north of the road.

Pay careful attention to your exposure here. The automatic exposure setting in some cameras can produce photos that are too dark, so you may need to override that setting to intentionally overexpose by ⅓ to one stop. At the same time, you need to be careful not to overexpose too much or you'll lose the detail in the salt.

48 Devil's Golf Course (West Side Road)

Mile 2.8, West Side Road

I prefer to photograph the Devil's Golf Course here, rather than the "official" location described on p. 85, because it doesn't get as many visitors. Without all that foot traffic, the wind- and water-sculpted salt shapes are more likely to be intact, and you can concentrate on shooting the best composition without worrying about cars or people in the background. Except for your own car, of course.

49 Eagle Borax Works

Mile 12.6, West Side Road

At this site, Isadore Daunet tried and failed to make his fortune refining borax. Little remains of the refinery operation, but there is an interpretive sign that explains how it worked. The real attraction here is the small marshy area, with cattails and yerba mansa providing habitat for marsh-nesting birds. You'll be shooting the marsh from the west, so you'll have direct light in the afternoon and nice backlighting on the cattails in early morning. Dragonflies and other insects are abundant here, too.

Other locations on West Side Road

If you have the time, there are many more places to stop and shoot along West Side Road. Some are historic sites, such as Bennet's Long Camp, where the Bennet and Arcan families, part of the original "lost 49ers," waited for nearly a month while William Lewis Manly and John Rogers walked to San Fernando, eventually returning with food and a route to safety. After only a few minutes in this spot, it's hard to imagine camping here with little or no food, not knowing if your companions will ever return.

Other locations along the road, identified by signs, include Tule Spring, Shorty's Well, and Shorty's Grave, any one of which can be a good place to explore among the small springs and clusters of mesquites.

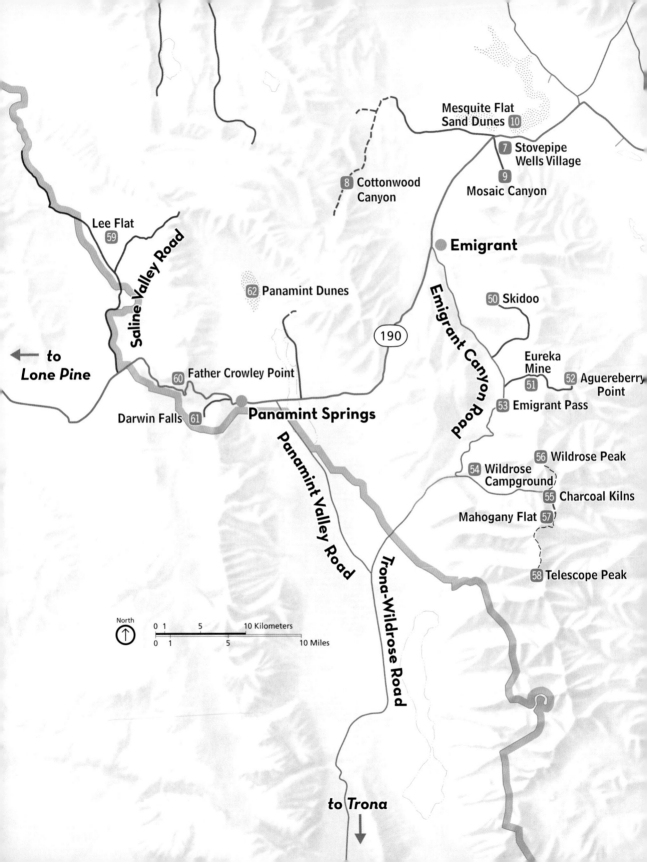

Mesquite Flat
Sand Dunes [10]

[7] Stovepipe
Wells Village

[8] Cottonwood
Canyon

[9] Mosaic Canyon

Lee Flat
[59]

● **Emigrant**

Saline Valley Road

[62] Panamint Dunes

[50] Skidoo

190

to
Lone Pine

Emigrant Canyon Road

[60] Father Crowley Point

Eureka
Mine

[52] Aguereberry
Point

[51]

Darwin Falls [61]

Panamint Springs

[53] Emigrant Pass

[56] Wildrose Peak

[54] Wildrose
Campground

[55] Charcoal Kilns

Mahogany Flat [57]

Panamint Valley Road

Trona-Wildrose Road

[58] Telescope Peak

North
↑

0 1   5   10 Kilometers

0 1   5   10 Miles

to Trona
↓

West

The western section of the park includes the historic Panamint Mountains and the northern end of Panamint Valley. Gas, food, and lodging are available at Stovepipe Wells Village and Panamint Springs. Campgrounds are located at Emigrant, Panamint Springs, and Wildrose Canyon. Restrooms can be found at the campgrounds and at Father Crowley Point. Outside the park, the nearest facilities are in Lone Pine and Trona.

Panamint Mountains

Once an important gold mining area, the Panamints are now a place to appreciate Death Valley's history as well as a great location for off-trail hiking.

50 Skidoo

Highlights: Ruins of mining operations, panoramic views
Flowers: April–May
Best light: Early morning, late afternoon
Elevation: 5,700'
Access: 8-mile dirt road; vehicles longer than 25 feet prohibited

If you're looking for a ghost town here, you might be disappointed, as were the four German tourists I met recently when they asked me for directions to Skidoo. They were surprised to find out it was all around them. No buildings remain of the town that once had 700 residents. The hundreds of mines produced about $1.6 million in gold over ten years—at a time when gold sold for just $20 an ounce—making Skidoo one of the richest mining camps in California. There are still dozens of open mineshafts here; use common sense and stay out of them.

What you will find here are a few remaining timbers around mine entrances, plus some of the trash those miners left behind: bedsprings, piles of tin cans and corrugated metal, even a car or two. Photographing those remains of an earlier time, in a stark landscape with no other sign of human occupation, conveys the harshness of life here.

At the interpretive sign in "downtown Skidoo" the road forks, the start of a network of interconnected roads in varying conditions, some of which may require a sturdy four-wheel-drive vehicle. Remnants of the mining operations, and other photo subjects, can be found along any of the roads. For an overview of the area, keep to the right and continue to the top of the hill.

Directions: From Stovepipe Wells Village, SW on SR190 for 9 miles; turn left on Emigrant Canyon Road for about 9.5 miles; turn left at the dirt road toward Skidoo for another 7 to 8 miles.

51 Eureka Mine and Aguereberry Camp

Highlights: Ruins of old mining operation
Flowers: April–May
Best light: Late afternoon
Elevation: 5,100'
Access: 2-mile dirt road; vehicles longer than 25 feet prohibited

The remains of an old car at Skidoo. To determine the exposure I spot metered on the hillside behind the car. Then I set my flash to underexpose by 1 stop, to avoid making the car's interior too bright. DSLR, 10-24mm lens at 13mm, 1/200 sec, f14, ISO 200.

This is the location described on p. 33, where Shorty Harris and Pete Aguereberry found gold in 1905. Shorty tried to take credit for the discovery, but Pete stayed and worked the mine for forty years, long after the boom-town had disappeared. In a bit of poetic justice, the site of the former Harrisburg is now known as Aguereberry Camp.

At Aguereberry Camp there's a turnout just big enough for two cars. Spend some time shooting Pete's house, then continue driving to the Eureka Mine another half mile up the road.

The best time to shoot here is late afternoon. From the parking area, walk to the west around the base of the hill, past the Cashier Mill and then up to the top of the hill for some views of wooden timbers, remnants of the mining operations, and some scary-looking holes you can fall into if you're not careful.

When you photograph the mill from this direction, you'll be looking back toward the parking area, so you might want to park your car a little farther down the road to keep it out of your photos. From the top of this hill you can also look down on Aguereberry Camp.

Directions: From Stovepipe Wells Village, SW on SR190 for 9 miles; turn left on Emigrant Canyon Road for about 12 miles; turn left at the dirt road toward Aguereberry Point for about 1.7 miles; turn right at the cutoff for Eureka Mine.

52 Aguereberry Point

Highlights: Panoramic view of Death Valley, hiking, flowers
Flowers: April–June
Best light: Early morning, late afternoon
Elevation: 6,433'
Access: 6-mile dirt road, steep for the last half mile; vehicles longer than 25 feet prohibited; short hike to the overlook

Almost a thousand feet higher than Dante's View, Aguereberry Point offers a good view of Death Valley from the west. From this vantage point, you can photograph the western face of the Amargosa Range. The only problem—and I hate to complain—is that you don't get a complete view of Death Valley. You can see the northern half of the valley and part of the south, but the middle is blocked by Tucki Mountain. (For an unobstructed view from this side of the valley, you need to do some serious hiking. See Wildrose Peak, p. 102, or Telescope Peak, p. 103.)

Just when the setting sun is doing its magic on the colors of the Amargosas, a deep shadow moves up on Tucki Mountain, dominating the foreground. Don't ignore that shadow; use it to make a dramatic composition.

The jagged rocks along the trail to the overlook are at their most photogenic in late afternoon or early morning light, especially with a full moon in the shot. And the overlook itself is a great place to watch the sunrise. In many years the road to Aguereberry Point can be a productive area to look for wildflowers.

Directions: From Stovepipe Wells Village, SW on SR190 for 9 miles; turn left on Emigrant Canyon Road for about 12 miles; turn left at the dirt road toward Aguereberry Point for about 6 miles, going straight at the cutoff for Eureka Mine. The trail to the overlook starts to the left of the big rock outcrop.

53 Emigrant Pass

Highlights: Flowers, views
Flowers: April–May
Best light: Late afternoon
Elevation: 5,318'
Access: Paved road

Driving through Emigrant Pass at midday, you might not think to stop here. Just before sunset, however, the broad pass and surrounding peaks light up with a warm red glow. It's even better during wildflower season, and if you can include the moon in the photo you'll really have something special.

Drive carefully in this area, for your own safety as well as to protect the local wildlife. I've seen more snakes crossing the road here than anywhere else in the park.

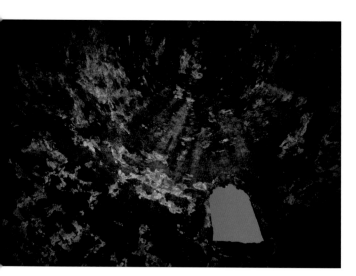

An inside view of a charcoal kiln in Wildrose Canyon. For this shot I spot metered on the sky through the window, then used two flashes at full power to light the blackened interior of the kiln. DSLR, 10-24mm lens at 10mm, 1/250 sec, f8, ISO 200.

Directions: From Stovepipe Wells Village, SW on SR190 for 9 miles; turn left on Emigrant Canyon Road for about 13 miles.

Wildrose Canyon

Wildrose Canyon, on the west side of the park, has a little of everything—wildflowers, birds, reptiles, mammals, historic sites, and spectacular views. From Panamint Valley you can drive the entire length of the canyon, starting near sea level and climbing to over 8,000 feet, passing through a variety of desert habitats along the way.

There are three campgrounds in the canyon: Wildrose, Thorndike, and Mahogany Flat. Pit toilets are located at each of the campgrounds and at the Charcoal Kilns.

54 Wildrose Campground

Highlights: Flowers, birds, wildlife
Flowers: March–May
Best light: Late afternoon
Elevation: 4,100'
Access: Paved road

Many people treat Wildrose Campground as a quick stopover on the way to somewhere else. In fact, I recently heard a ranger tell someone it was a place to arrive late and leave early. But Wildrose is more than just a convenient place to camp when the valley floor is too hot. The late afternoon light here is simply beautiful.

Hike up the hills above the campground just before sunset and watch as the whole canyon is bathed in a warm red glow. To the west, the sky over Panamint Valley and the Argus Range becomes a constantly changing light show of red, orange, and pink. Morning light here feels more leisurely, as the sun doesn't rise over Telescope Peak until long after dawn.

Chuckwallas and collared lizards are common on the rocky slopes above the campground, and whiptail and side-blotched lizards can often be seen in the campsites. Desert cottontails are also common here, especially just before sunrise and after sunset as they scamper from one bush to the next, somehow always staying at the edges of your field of vision. Get up early and watch their traffic patterns before choosing a place to shoot; then sit quietly with your camera ready, and you should be able to get a good photo or two.

The two major springs—the larger one between the two roads below the campground, and the smaller one at the upper end of the campground—are good birding locations, attracting warblers, finches, orioles, quail, and other species. Be careful, especially around the lower spring—rattlesnakes are very common here, and could be hiding in the brush between the spring and the road. Don't step where you can't see your feet.

In a good year the wildflowers here can be fantastic. Even in a not-so-good year the elevation range means you should be able to find something blooming along this road. About 2 miles below the campground, on the north side of Trona-Wildrose Road, is a wash where you might find a stand of Panamint daisies. Their large, gaudy blooms seem to defy the arid conditions they thrive on. And if the daisies aren't blooming, don't worry—the dry, wilted plants have their own special beauty. For added drama, lie down and shoot the plant against the sky, or backlit against a dark background. Above the campground, prince's plume lines the road, and in most years you can find desert mariposa, Mojave aster, langloisia, prickly poppy, and other flowers.

Directions: At the junction of Emigrant Canyon Road and Trona-Wildrose Road.

Caution: The 4-mile stretch of Trona-Wildrose Road just below the campground is unpaved and can be rough at times. If you don't have a high-clearance vehicle, use Emigrant Canyon Road.

55 Charcoal Kilns

Highlights: Charcoal kilns, reptiles
Flowers: April–June
Best light: Late afternoon
Elevation: 6,800'
Access: 8-mile gravel road, conditions vary

At the upper end of Wildrose Canyon is a row of ten enormous, beehive-shaped stone kilns that were once used to make charcoal for a silver and lead smelting operation in the Argus Range, west of Panamint Valley. Built in the 1870s by the Modock Consolidated Mining Company (whose owners included George Hearst, the future U.S. Senator and father of publisher William Randolph Hearst), the kilns were used only for about three years. These are considered the best-preserved charcoal kilns in the West.

Charcoal was a preferred source of fuel because its high carbon content produces the high temperatures needed for smelting. Each batch of charcoal took up to two weeks to make. First the kilns were packed with piñon pine logs, which were ignited and left to burn for six to eight days. Cooling took another five days, and then the charcoal was loaded onto wagons for the 25-mile trek to the smelters.

The shapes, shadows, and textures of the stone kilns provide endless photo opportunities. Climb the hill behind the kilns for a wider view that includes Wildrose Canyon, or shoot from the road with a longer lens to compress the perspective and make the kilns appear closer together. Looking up from ground level at a single kiln can make a dramatic photo, or you could simply move in close and concentrate on the texture of the stone. Or shoot from inside a kiln, looking out at the canyon…again, the possibilities are endless.

Directions: 8 miles E of Wildrose Campground on Mahogany Flat Road.

56 Wildrose Peak

Highlights: Views of Wildrose Canyon
   and Death Valley, hiking
Flowers: April–June
Best light: Early morning, late afternoon
Elevation: 6,800 to 9,064'
Access: 8-mile gravel road; moderately
   strenuous 8.5-mile hike (round trip)

This trail passes through a piñon-juniper woodland and offers views of both Wildrose Canyon and Death Valley. The hike starts at the lower end of the Charcoal Kilns, and for the first mile it's a pretty easy walk (after the initial climb up the hill from the kilns). If you're looking for a good place to watch the sun set over Wildrose Canyon, this is it.

Farther along, the trail gets steeper and crosses a saddle to the east. Now the views are of Death Valley, and the higher you go, the better those views get. The last mile or so is all switchbacks as you climb to the summit. Count on strong winds at the summit, along with views that stretch all the way to the Amargosa Range to the east and the Sierra Nevada to the west. To the south, you'll be looking up at Telescope Peak (p. 103). If you

like this hike, you'll love the hike to Telescope.

From about December through April there could be snow on the trail—more in some years, very little in others.

Directions: Trail starts at the lower end of the Charcoal Kilns, 8 miles E of Wildrose Campground via Mahogany Flat Road.

57 Mahogany Flat and
Thorndike Campgrounds

Highlights: View of Death Valley, birds,
   trees
Flowers: May–June
Best light: Early morning, late afternoon
Elevation: Mahogany Flat 8,200',
   Thorndike 7,400'
Access: 10-mile gravel road; may be
   rough; may be closed by snow

The highest campgrounds in the park, Mahogany Flat and Thorndike are popular fall camping destinations. Both are located in the piñon-juniper woodland at the upper end of Wildrose Canyon. Wildlife here may not be as abundant as at the springs near Wildrose Campground, but you'll still see lizards and birds. Deer and bighorn sheep may occasionally be seen here as well.

I prefer Mahogany Flat for its views of Death Valley and the trailhead to Telescope Peak. I usually think of Thorndike as the second choice, when Mahogany Flat is full or the road is in especially bad shape.

It's hard to predict the condition of the road from the Charcoal Kilns. Some years I've seen it smooth and easily passable in a passenger car, while at other times it's washed out by spring snowmelt and a challenge for even the best four-wheel-drive vehicle.

Directions: 10 miles E of Wildrose Campground via Mahogany Flat Road.

58 Telescope Peak

Highlights: Panoramic views of Death Valley, hiking
Flowers: May–July
Best light: Early morning, late afternoon
Elevation: 8,200 to 11,049'
Access: 10-mile gravel road; may be rough; may be closed by snow; 14-mile hike (round trip)

This is a long and strenuous hike, but the views along the trail and from Telescope Peak—the highest point in the park—make it worth the effort. In winter and early spring it should be attempted only by experienced climbers with appropriate winter climbing equipment. For the rest of us it's a good all-day hike in summer or fall.

As you gain elevation, the piñons and junipers give way to bristlecones and limber pines. The twisted, gnarled shapes of the bristlecones provide dramatic photo possibilities, especially early in the morning. It's best to start hiking as early as possible and pay attention to the time. If you stop for too many photos, you might not have time to reach the peak and get back before dark.

Directions: Trail starts at Mahogany Flat Campground, 10 miles E of Wildrose Campground.

Darwin Falls provides habitat for many birds and insects, as well as respite from the desert heat. To show movement in the flowing water, experiment with shutter speeds between 1/30 and 1 second. DSLR, 18-70mm lens at 25mm, 1/10 sec, f22, ISO 100.

Panamint Valley

In 1994, thanks to the dedication and persistence of Senator Dianne Feinstein, Congress passed the California Desert Protection Act, which upgraded Death Valley from a national monument to a national park. At the same time, the park boundaries were extended to include the northern end of Panamint Valley, giving protection to several important natural features.

59 Lee Flat

Highlights: Joshua trees, reptiles
Flowers: April–May
Best light: Early morning, late afternoon
Elevation: 5,400'
Access: 8- to 10-mile gravel road

Lee Flat is often described as the best Joshua tree location in the park, a broad valley with Joshua trees as far as you can see in all directions. With careful planning, you can shoot the sun rising or setting through a forest of Joshua trees. A telephoto lens will compress the perspective and make the Joshua trees appear denser and closer together, as well as making the sun larger in the frame.

Because of its orientation, running roughly northwest to southeast, Lee Flat has better light in the early morning. For the best late afternoon light, go right at the fork in the road to avoid the shadow of the mountains to the west.

The last time I drove this road it was in the worst possible condition: deteriorating pavement alternating with washboard gravel, soft dirt, sand, and everything in between, with foot-deep potholes and abrupt transitions that can do serious damage to your tires, your suspension, and your kidneys. Unless the road has been fixed since then, you should plan on at least a half hour to get to Lee Flat from the highway.

Directions: From Panamint Springs, W on SR 190 for 13 miles; turn right on Saline Valley Road for about 8 miles, then go either direction when the road forks. The Joshua trees will be all around you.

60 Father Crowley Point

Highlights: Views of Panamint Valley
**   and Rainbow Canyon**
Flowers: April–May
Best light: Early morning, late afternoon
Elevation: 4,200'
Access: Paved road

Father John Crowley was a Catholic priest whose parish in the 1920s covered 30,000 square miles from Bishop to Barstow. He was well loved by miners and others throughout the region. Later, when water diversions by the city of Los Angeles had destroyed most agriculture in the Owens Valley, he was instrumental in developing a tourist economy in that area.

The overlook that bears his name has no particular historic significance, but was said to be one of his favorite places to take a break and enjoy the view. The parking area provides a view of Rainbow Canyon, its rich colors standing in contrast to the surrounding dark lava flows. The best light here is at

sunrise, especially in spring and fall, when the rising sun aligns with the direction of the canyon.

At the eastern end of the parking lot, a ¼-mile dirt road leads to another overlook with an even bigger view. (The road can be pretty rough—it's usually best to walk, not drive.) From here you see the flat, pale lakebed of Panamint Valley, with the dunes sitting high on the alluvial fan at the north-

A slightly overcast sky gives a delicate softness to the light on the Panamint Dunes. 35mm Fujichrome Velvia 50 film, ISO 50, lens and exposure data not recorded.

ern end, while directly in front of you the highway snakes along in what looks like a scene from a car commercial. The best light on the valley will be in late afternoon, but not too late because the mountains you're standing on will cast a shadow as the sun

When shooting sand dunes, remember to use a longer lens to isolate interesting details in the shadows. 35mm Ektachrome 64X film, 70-300mm lens, ISO 64, focal length and exposure data not recorded.

moves behind them. It's also a great place to watch the sun rise.

Directions: 7 miles W of Panamint Springs on SR190.

61 Darwin Falls

Highlights: Waterfall, birds, reptiles, hiking, shade
Flowers: March–May
Best light: Early morning
Elevation: 2,800'
Access: 3-mile gravel road; 2-mile hike (round trip)

This distinctive forked waterfall flows year-round, although in some summers it's not much more than a trickle. Not only is it beautiful and unexpected, there's an extra bonus as well: hiking into this tree-lined, water-cooled canyon is a welcome respite from the desert heat. It's a great spot to break for lunch, or just to sit for an hour and enjoy the cool breeze before heading back out into the sun. As you hike up the canyon, you'll cross the creek a couple times, so be prepared to get your feet wet.

The willows and cattails along the creek provide refuge to a variety of birds, especially in springtime, and a brilliant red dragonfly called the flame skimmer. The creek below the falls is home to a population of western toads; you can sometimes find their eggs or tadpoles in the shallow water.

Conditions change from year to year and season to season. Sometimes the pool below the falls is big enough to swim (or at least wade) in, and other times it's just a puddle. Depending on the vegetation, you might be able to approach the falls from different angles, or your vantage point might be more restricted. To shoot the falls, make sure you bring a tripod so you can experiment with slow shutter speeds. Depending on the effect you want, anywhere between 1/15 and one second will result in a nice blurring of the falling water.

The trail that continues up the canyon to the left of the falls is not for the inexperienced climber or faint of heart. I've been there a couple times, but that was enough. Negotiating the sheer cliffs and narrow ledges with a heavy camera bag is just too dangerous.

Directions: From Panamint Springs, W on SR190 for 1 mile; turn left onto the unmarked gravel road for 3 miles; parking area is on the right. Hike up the canyon about 1 mile.

62 Panamint Dunes

Highlights: Sand dunes, reptiles, hiking
Flowers: March–April
Best light: Early morning, late afternoon
Elevation: 2,400'
Access: 6-mile rough dirt road, may
    require 4WD; 6-mile hike (round trip)
    plus hiking on the dunes

Kangaroo rats are mostly nocturnal but may occasionally be seen in the daytime. DSLR, 70-300mm lens at 300mm, 1/500 sec, f8, ISO 200.

Driving north on Panamint Valley Road, you see a strange sight ahead of you—sand dunes that seem to float above the valley, sitting high on an alluvial fan that appears to reach halfway up the mountain. These are the Panamint Dunes, one of the more photogenic dune systems in the park.

Their location, on the lower slope of Hunter Mountain almost a thousand feet above the floor of Panamint Valley, gives these dunes a vantage point unlike any others I know of. In the morning and evening you can shoot the dunes against the dramatic backdrop of Hunter Mountain. You can also point your camera in the other direction, with the broad expanse of Panamint Valley as a background.

For the best light, start hiking well before sunrise; you might want to spend the previous night at the nearby Panamint Springs Resort. Or, to shoot the evening light, hike out in the afternoon and stay late; just don't forget your flashlight. As you hike across the sandy area before the dunes, you'll find abundant jackrabbits, desert iguanas, and other lizards, as well as an occasional sidewinder.

On the drive out to the parking area you pass Lake Hill, on the west side of the road, where you might find spiny lizards and other rock-dwelling lizards, followed by a seasonal lakebed that in spring can have a beautiful display of wildflowers. Shoot the lakebed from the north, with the dark rocky hills looming above it, for a dramatic contrast.

The road to the dunes crosses several washes and may be impassable in wet weather. Even in dry weather it's a pretty slow drive—on my last visit it took a half hour to go six miles.

Directions: From Panamint Springs, E on SR190 for 4.5 miles; turn left on the dirt road for about 6 miles to the parking area.

Location chart and index

Location	Page	Map #	Elevation	Flowers	Morn. light
Aguereberry Camp	97	51	5,000	Apr–May	
Aguereberry Point	99	52	6,433	Apr–Jun	●
Artist's Drive and Artist's Palette	85	32	800	Feb–Mar	
Ash Meadows	81	29	2,300	Mar–Apr	●
Ashford Mill	88	37	-100	Feb–Mar	●
Badwater	86	35	-282	Not likely	
Bottle House	65	14	3,800	Apr–May	●
Butte Valley	93	45	3,700	Apr–May	●
Charcoal Kilns	101	55	6,800	Apr–Jun	
Cottonwood Canyon	61	8	2,000	Apr–May	●
Dante's View	79	27	5,475	Apr–Jun	●
Darwin Falls	106	61	2,800	Mar–May	●
Devil's Cornfield	64	11	0	Feb–Mar	●
Devil's Golf Course (Badwater Road)	85	33	-200	Not likely	●
Devil's Golf Course (West Side Road)	95	48	-200	Not likely	●
Eagle Borax Works	95	49	-200	Feb–Apr	●
Emigrant Pass	99	53	5,318	Apr–May	
Eureka Dunes	54	2	3,500	Mar–Apr	●
Eureka Mine	97	51	5,100	Apr–May	
Father Crowley Point	104	60	4,200	Apr–May	●
Furnace Creek	77	24	-200	Feb–Mar	
Golden Canyon	82	30	0	Feb–Mar	

Eve. light	Birds	History	Sand Dunes	Notes	Access
•		•		Old mining camp	Dirt road; no trailers
•				Good flower location	Dirt road; no trailers
•				Colorful geology	Paved road; no trailers
•	•			Springs	Gravel road
•		•		Ruins	Dirt road
•				Lowest point in N. America	Paved road, walk to salt flats
•		•		50,000 bottles	Paved road
•		•		Old cabins	4WD; closed in summer
•		•		Huge beehive-shaped kilns	Gravel road
				Good off-trail hiking	4WD; may be closed in summer
				Panoramic views	Paved road; no trailers
	•			Waterfall	Gravel road, hiking
•				Weird plants	Paved road
•				Eroded salt formations	Dirt road
•				Eroded salt formations	Gravel road
•	•	•		Marsh	Gravel road
•				Beautiful evening light	Paved road
•			•	Endangered plants	Gravel road
•		•		Ruins of old mill	Dirt road; no trailers
•				Panoramic views	Paved road
•	•	•		Food, gas, lodging	Paved road
•				Hike to Zabriskie Point	Paved road, hiking

Location	Page	Map #	Elevation	Flowers	Morn. light
Goldwell Museum	65	14	3,800	Apr–May	●
Greenwater Valley	81	28	Various	Mar–May	●
Hanaupah Canyon	92	43	5,000	Mar–May	●
Harmony Borax Works	75	22	-200	Feb–Mar	●
Historic Stovepipe Well	64	12	0	Feb–Mar	●
Ibex Dunes	90	41	400	Feb–Apr	●
Joshua Flats	53	1	6,100	Apr–May	●
Jubilee Pass	88	38	1,290	Mar–May	
Klare Spring	71	20	3,200	Mar–May	
Leadfield	70	19	4,000	Apr–May	
Lee Flat	104	59	5,400	Apr–May	●
Mahogany Flat Campground	102	57	8,200	May–Jun	●
Mesquite Flat Sand Dunes	63	10	0	Feb–Mar	●
Mormon Point	87	36	-200	Feb–Mar	
Mosaic Canyon	62	9	1,000	Feb–Mar	
Mushroom Rock	83	31	-200	Feb–Mar	
Mustard Canyon	75	23	-200	Feb–Mar	●
Natural Bridge	86	34	1,000	Feb–Mar	
Panamint Dunes	107	62	2,400	Mar–Apr	●
Panamint Mountains	97	50–53	Various	Apr–Jun	●
Panamint Valley	104	59–62	Various	Mar–May	●
Racetrack	58	5	3,700	Mar–Apr	●
Red Pass	68	17	5,250	Apr–Jun	●
Rhyolite	65	14	3,800	Apr–May	●

Eve. light	Birds	History	Sand Dunes	Notes	Access
•				Outdoor sculptures	Paved road
•				Good flower location	Dirt road
	•			Waterfalls	4WD; closed in summer
•		•		Borax wagon	Dirt road, easy walk
•		•		Hike to sand dunes	Dirt road
•			•	Beautiful evening light	Dirt road, off-trail hiking
•				Joshua trees	Paved or gravel roads
•				Good flower location	Paved road
•		•		Petroglyphs	Dirt road
•		•		Ghost town	Dirt road
•				Joshua trees	Gravel road
•	•			Panoramic views	Gravel road; closed in winter
•			•	Easiest access to dunes	Paved road, hiking
•				Good flower location	Paved road
				Marble	Gravel road, hiking
•				Good flower location	Paved road
•				Colorful canyon	Dirt road
•				Geology	Gravel road, hiking
•			•	Dunes with a view	Rough dirt road, hiking
•				See specific locations	See specific locations
•	•		•	See specific locations	See specific locations
•				Moving rocks	Rough gravel road
				Panoramic views	Dirt road
•		•		Ghost town	Paved road

Location	Page	Map #	Elevation	Flowers	Morn. light
Salsberry Pass	88	39	3,315	Apr–May	●
Salt Creek Hills	91	42	600	Feb–Mar	
Salt Creek Interpretive Trail	65	13	-200	Feb–Mar	●
Salt Flats (West Side Road)	94	47	-200	Not likely	●
Saratoga Spring	89	40	200	Feb–Apr	
Scotty's Castle	57	3	3,000	Mar–Apr	
Skidoo	97	50	5,700	Apr–May	●
Stovepipe Well (historic site)	64	12	0	Feb–Mar	●
Stovepipe Wells Village	61	7	0	Feb–Mar	●
Teakettle Junction	58	6	4,200	Mar–Apr	●
Telescope Peak	103	58	11,049	May–Jul	●
Thimble Peak	69	18	6,381	Apr–Jun	●
Thorndike Campground	102	57	7,400	May–Jun	
Titus Canyon Narrows	72	21	1,000	Feb–Apr	
Titus Canyon Road	67	15–21	Various	Mar–Jun	●
Twenty Mule Team Canyon	78	26	1,000	Not likely	●
Ubehebe Crater	58	4	2,500	Not likely	●
Warm Spring Canyon	93	44	2,600	Mar–May	●
West Side Road	94	46–49	-200	Feb–Mar	●
White Pass	68	16	5,100	Apr–Jun	●
Wildrose Campground	100	54	4,100	Mar–May	
Wildrose Canyon	100	54–58	Various	Mar–Jun	
Wildrose Peak	102	56	9,064	Apr–Jun	●
Zabriskie Point	77	25	700	Not likely	●

Eve. light	Birds	History	Sand Dunes	Notes	Access
●				Panoramic views	Paved road
●	●			Spring & marsh	Paved road, short walk
●	●			Pupfish	Dirt road, boardwalk
●				Mosaic patterns in salt	Gravel road
●	●			Spring & marsh	Dirt road, walk to spring
●	●	●		Architecture	Paved road
●		●		Ruins of mines	Dirt road; no trailers
●		●		Hike to sand dunes	Dirt road
	●	●		Food, gas, lodging	Paved roads
●				Bring a teakettle	Rough gravel road
●				Panoramic views	Gravel, long hike; closed winter
●				Panoramic views	Dirt road, hiking
●	●			High elevation camping	Gravel road; closed in winter
				Geology	Dirt road
●		●		See specific locations	Dirt road
●				Colorful badlands	Dirt road
●				Huge crater	Paved road, hiking
	●	●		Good flower location	Dirt road; closed in summer
●	●	●		See specific locations	Gravel road
				Panoramic views	Dirt road
●	●			Good flower location	Paved road
●	●	●		See specific locations	Gravel road
●				Panoramic views	Gravel road, hiking
●				Colorful badlands	Paved road, short walk

Resources

Park information

Death Valley National Park
www.nps.gov/deva
760-786-3200

Death Valley Natural History Association
www.dvnha.org
760-786-2146

Ash Meadows National Wildlife Refuge
www.fws.gov/desertcomplex/
    ashmeadows
775-372-5435

Lodging in the park

Furnace Creek Inn and Ranch
www.furnacecreekresort.com
760-786-2345

Panamint Springs Resort
www.deathvalley.com/psr
775-482-7680

Stovepipe Wells Village
www.escapetodeathvalley.com
760-786-2387

Recommended books

Death Valley and the Amargosa, A Land of Illusion by Richard Lingenfelter
Death Valley Wildflowers by Roxanna Ferris
Field Guide to Birds of Western North America by David Allen Sibley
Field Guide to Western Reptiles and Amphibians by Robert Stebbins
Geology of Death Valley National Park by Marli Miller and Lauren Wright
The Jepson Desert Manual: Vascular Plants of Southeastern California by Bruce G. Baldwin et al.
Mammals of California by E. W. Jameson and Hans Peeters

Maps

Tom Harrison Maps
www.tomharrisonmaps.com

Trails Illustrated Maps
www.natgeomaps.com/
    trailsillustrated.html

Online resources

For updated links to:

Road conditions
Wildflower reports
Wildlife checklists
Books and maps
Lodging and tours
Camera and lens reviews
Photoshop techniques
Technical advice
Useful gadgets

Visit
www.DeathValleyPhotographersGuide.com